ORAL INTERPRETATION OF CHILDREN'S LITERATURE

ORAL INTERPRETATION OF CHILDREN'S LITERATURE

SECOND EDITION

Henry A. Bamman
Mildred A. Dawson
Robert J. Whitehead

Sacramento State College

WM. C. BROWN COMPANY PUBLISHERS
Dubuque, Iowa

Contents

Preface

This book about children and their oral interpretation of literature is not intended to be an exhaustive reference source on either of these two subjects; rather, it is intended to be a concise and informative guide to the principles, techniques, and materials available for aiding children to learn to express themselves happily and effectively through the medium of literature. The book is designed to give teachers, children, and parents practical help with this important facet of school and family life.

Good oral interpretation of literature is not something remote from the everyday lives of children; it is a natural extension of the child's desire to express himself and to communicate with others; it is a contributor to children's genuine enjoyment and appreciation of the whole body of good literature. For children in the elementary school, a good book often needs more than just a sound plot and interesting characters. It needs the voice of a teacher or a parent—vital, warm, expressive—to transport the child-listener into the book or the poem itself; to stir his emotions and stimulate his mind; and to make the characters and scenes as real as the people and places that are so familiar to him in his own life.

This second edition—an expanded and refined version of the first edition of this book—includes steps for teaching choral speaking, for reading prose and poetry aloud, for dramatization, and for storytelling. Procedures, suggestions, and materials are given for challenging the adult reader, as well as the children at all elementary school levels. These techniques and source lists have grown out of years of experience that the authors have enjoyed with children and children's literature. It is hoped that in sharing these ideas with teachers and parents, we have directly aided children in becoming more adequately equipped with those attitudes and skills which will open up avenues of greater appreciation for the literature that has been written for them. The children that we know have infinite capacities for enjoying good literature. As they develop discrimination in the selection of worthwhile literature, attitudes that deepen their enjoyment of literature, and skills in communicating literature to others, their lives may be immeasurably enriched.

Henry A. Bamman
Mildred A. Dawson
Robert J. Whitehead

CHAPTER

1

How to Read Orally

The writer could "read" when she entered school at the age of five and read the first page of the old *Barnes First Reader* with ease on the first day of school. In a high-pitched, monotonous voice she chanted:

It   is   a   dog.
The   dog   can   run.

She spoke one word at a time, never once thinking of a dog. She simply saw some individual printed words and mouthed each one, whereas she should have interpreted the meaning of each sentence in the light of her experience and earlier learnings and should have read each sentence in a natural, conversational manner.

Little Margery was the brightest girl in her class and read silently with phenomenal speed and real understanding. She read orally as fast as it was possible to enunciate the words. She rattled off the stories she read aloud so rapidly that her listeners missed almost every idea she was reading. She, too, was not actually doing oral reading, which is a reader's communication of a writer's message with as much meaning and as genuine an emotional reaction as the author himself would convey if he were present and speaking.

Many adults read aloud poorly and fail to make clear the thoughts that the writer is expressing. This is especially true in the oral reading of poetry. Any singsong effect causes the exaggerated rhythm to get in the way of meaning; or unwarranted pauses at the end of lines without punctuation break up sentences in such a way as to conceal the ideas. For instance, in the following poem there should be no stop at the end of lines 1, 3, 7, and 9 if meaning is not to become confused, since the phrasing in these parts of the poem should be as follows:

> and wish that I could be a kite up in the sky
> and go whatever way it chanced to blow
> that sail like me before the merry gale
> I came to some place with a foreign name

This is the poem:

A KITE

I often sit and wish that I
Could be a kite up in the sky,
And ride upon the breeze and go
Whatever way it chanced to blow;
Then I could look beyond the town
And see the river winding down,
And follow all the ships that sail
Like me before the merry gale,
Until at last with them I came
To some place with a foreign name.

Unknown

Poetry is intended for the ear and should be heard. The reading should be fluent, meaningful, musical, true to the mood which the poet intended. Even as gifted and experienced a reader as the noted Charles Laughton wanted the opportunity to prepare for his oral reading. Usually it is the *teacher* who should read a poem to the class, and then only after looking it over and possibly rehearsing it orally, so as to make sure of getting the best effects. She should make a decided effort to determine the tone of voice, the rate of reading, the emphasis on words that will truly reflect the mood and convey the meanings which the poet tried to express.

Situations Involving Oral Reading

An intrinsic part of regular reading instruction is the oral reading contained in the typical reading lesson. This book is not concerned with that phase of oral reading. Only reading aloud by the children or their teacher, as a means of presenting and interpreting literature, is to be considered here. There are three general situations which will be discussed: sight reading, audience situations, and practice on the skills implicit in effective oral reading.

Sight Reading

By sight reading is meant oral reading of materials that are completely new to the reader; he has never seen them before. Some authorities recommend that there be absolutely no sight reading in the elementary school, that there always be definite preparation beforehand by study or at least by a silent perusal. However, because some precocious readers register an unusually high level of reading achievement, such a stringent ban seems unjustified. The following rule-of-thumb works pretty well: Knowing what the instructional reading level of a child is, you should subtract "two years"; that is, if a fifth-grade pupil is reading at eighth-grade level, he can probably read sixth-grade material at sight if it is relatively simple in structure and concept.

Even so, it is usually better to avoid sight reading. Adults who are experienced and expert oral readers generally prefer to go over selections to be read orally before making their presentation. The teacher should make a practice of planning ahead of time what materials she wants certain pupils to read aloud, and then she should definitely assign the portions to specific pupils who will carefully prepare what they are to read. Such reading is almost sure to be more effective than any sight reading. And too, listeners are more likely to understand and be interested.

Audience Situations

In an audience situation, a pupil reads aloud in order to entertain, inform, or convince one or more listeners. There is nothing routine about the reading he does. He is reading something he wants to share with others—something he believes they will enjoy hearing or will profit from hearing. (Rarely does such a true audience situation exist when the children take turns reading portions of a familiar story, one after another, as they do with selections from a basal reader.) Usually the materials are selected because of their beauty, their vividness or stirring nature, or their importance. They are something an audience looks forward to hearing.

The newer series of readers contain many literary selections of true merit. Oral reading can be used advantageously as one means of interpreting such selections. Each pupil should select a part that he has thoroughly enjoyed and believes his classmates will want to hear. For instance, these are some of the portions he will select:

Vivid word pictures
   Description of a character
   Description of a scene
   Account of lively or humorous action
Dialogue that reflects strong emotions
A portion he will ask his listeners to dramatize
A portion a class cartoonist may sketch

Most of the audience situations will utilize selected portions from a pupil's individual reading. He is sharing with his companions something he has enjoyed. Often he selects from a library book that he will "advertise" through oral reading so as to induce his friends to choose this book for their own next reading. Sometimes the teacher does the reading in order to call attention to a newly acquired book or to one that lies untouched on the shelf because the children do not realize how interesting it is.

Often a child will bring his materials from home. There may be a poem in a children's magazine, a favorite collection of fairy stories, a book recently received as a gift or one secured from his book club, or a book long treasured in the family. In such circumstances, the child has certain responsibilities: (1) to select a part that will intrigue his listeners; (2) to make careful preparation so that he can read well; and (3) to be an effective reader who interprets the ideas and feelings the author has attempted to portray.

Practice Lessons

One important aspect of an effective program for interpreting literature orally is the development of skills that will enable the best possible presentation of materials. Above the primary grades, there is need for a systematic series of lessons designed to build skills specifically called for in oral reading.

The first of the skills is the clear and distinct pronunciation of words. The second is the adjustment of rate of reading to suit the situation which the literature portrays. Similarly, the tone of voice should be suited to the emotional atmosphere of a selection; for instance, a state of excitement would call for a very different tone from one in which peaceful contentment or stealthy action prevails. In the effort to convey meanings—whether a major point or more subtly different details—the oral reader must be truly skillful in giving emphasis to key ideas through inflections and intonations of his voice, through strategic pauses, through perfect phrasing of words, and through artistic subordination of ideas. Such are the skills that are explained in the section to follow.

The Skills of Oral Reading

Clear and Distinct Enunciation

Americans are said to be lazy-tongued and lazy-lipped because they run so many words together, such as *gonna* for *going to* or *doncha* for *don't you*. Many people habitually leave the *g* off words ending in *ing*. Children need numerous lessons that will teach them to say each word separately and distinctly. Here are some types of exercises to help in improving enunciation and articulation of sounds.

Words that end in *d, t, b, p, k,* and hard *g* need a great deal of attention. It is possible to find little rhymes that contain many such words. These can be put on practice charts, the chalkboard, or dittoed copies. These two rhymes are good examples.

> There was an old owl who lived in an oak;
> The more he heard, the less he spoke.
> The less he spoke, the more he heard.
> Why aren't we like that wise old bird?
>
> *Traditional rhyme*

> A centipede was happy quite
> Until a frog in fun
> Said, "Pray, which leg comes after which?"
> This raised her mind to such a pitch,
> She lay distracted in the ditch
> Considering how to run.
>
> *Unknown*

When children are practicing on these critical word endings, have them slightly overemphasize the *d, t, b, p, k,* and hard *g* sounds. They will find this fun to do and are likely to become more alert to such endings when they read orally.

Sometimes the children are called on to read excerpts in which several successive words begin with the same sound, this alliteration causing them to stumble and stammer. Enjoyable practice materials for achieving clear and distinct reading of alliterative passages are provided by tongue twisters. "Peter Piper Picked a Peck" and "If a Woodchuck Would Chuck" are familiar examples of such tongue twisters. Here are two more.

> Tommy T. Tattamus took two T's
>   To tie his tups to two tall trees,
> To frighten the terrible Thomas T. Tattamus.
>   Tell us how many T's there are in all that.
>
> *Unknown*

Betty Botter bought some butter,
But she said, "This butter's bitter.
If I put it in my batter,
It will make my batter bitter,
But a bit of better butter
Will make my batter better."
So she bought a bit of butter,
Better than the bitter butter,
And it made her batter better.
So 'twas better Betty Botter
Bought a bit of better butter.

Unknown

On such tongue twisters the children should make a slow start so as to make each word a distinct unit. Gradually they may speed up, but with care to keep the words separate and clear.

A resourceful teacher can always make up sentences that contain critical sounds, whether at the beginning, the end, or the middle of words. Note the italicized letters in these sentences.

David dipped cold milk with a big, big dipper.
Peg would shrug at the pug dog's mug and leg.
Spatter, clatter, splatter came the rain and hail.

Rate of Reading

A highly competent reader varies his rate of oral reading to suit the action and mood of the situation which the words depict. Most selections will be read at a fairly uniform rate, always slowly enough for listeners to follow with ease and enjoyment. However, there may come passages which can be best interpreted by slowing down or accelerating the reading rate. Note these passages from the fables and famous folktales. Excerpt 1 calls for quiet-toned deliberate reading; excerpt 3, while slow, calls for more vigor; excerpts 2 and 4 should be read rapidly in staccato fashion.

Well, she sat as still as a mouse, moving neither hand nor foot, not even her eyes, and waited, and waited, and waited. . . . So she waited, and waited, and waited. Long she sat, and aye she wearied.

The cat flew into his face, spitting and scratching. Then he cried out in fright and ran toward the door, and the dog, who was lying there, bit the robber's leg.

The Tortoise plodded on and plodded on.

And so he flew at the Troll, and poked him and knocked him, and crushed him to bits, body and bones, and tossed him out into the burn.

Poets choose words and word-sounds that reflect mood and action, which likewise suggest the best rate of reading. Note how the rate of reading should change within this poem.

Ponderous and slow	Slowly ticks the big clock; Tick-tock, tick-tock!
Light and double-time	But cuckoo clock ticks a double quick; Tick-a-tock-a, tick-a-tock-a, tick-a-tock-a, tick!

Unknown

Or, take selected verses from Tennyson's "The Brook."

By thirty hills I hurry down,
Or slip between the ridges, . . .

I chatter over stony ways,
In little sharps and trebles,
I bubble into eddying bays,
I babble on the pebbles. . . .

I murmur under moon and stars
In brambly wildernesses;
I linger by my shingly bars,
I loiter round my cresses; . . .

Who could help but linger over the words of Walter de la Mare's "Silver" when its first words are: "Slowly, silently"? How restrained the pace and volume of speech must be in reading Elinor Wylie's "Velvet Shoes," which features "soundless space," "footsteps quiet and slow," and "a tranquil pace." And how differently does the good reader picture moving, as in the words of Eunice Tietjens, he portrays the "hurrying and scurrying" of the movers with their "hammering and tacking." Dorothy Baruch almost perfectly reflects the long wait of cars while the drivers wait for the green light, then make an instantaneous rush to get going again in her "Stop—Go."

To develop the skill of adjusting the rate at times when proper reading calls for a change, the children need to have practice in reading sentences and short quotations that definitely call for a particular rate of reading. It is easy to find such excerpts in readers having stories with passages that portray strong emotion, especially in the dialogue of characters who are deeply stirred. The nursery rhymes and poems to be found in anthologies may also be used after reproduction on charts, the chalkboard, or sheets of paper.

Too, the teacher can devise sentences that call for a variety of rates of reading. The children enjoy trying to give the most effective rendition. Here are some sample sentences:

Slowly and sadly they laid the dead bird to rest.

Quickly, trippingly the fairies danced.

Tinkle-tinkle went the silver bells; ding-dong clanged
the huge iron bells.

(The volume of the voice may likewise vary in terms of the emotion and situation that the words portray. Most of the illustrations used for showing how rate will vary may also be used to evoke a change in the volume of the voice. For instance, words that *roar* will be spoken more loudly and vigorously than those that *whisper*.)

Phrasing

One of the first skills that a child reader must learn is the linguistic one requiring him to so put together the words within sentences that they will become meaningful groups. Then pauses to get breath will not interrupt the thought. He should never be permitted to read word by word, to engage in word-calling. When he does his preliminary silent reading, he should seek the ideas that the words express, note the word-groupings or phrasing that will keep key ideas intact while allowing voice pauses to permit breathing, then read the sentences as if talking. By so doing, he is almost sure to stop in the right places so that his listeners can follow the ideas.

One exercise that may prove helpful is to place sentences on the chalkboard and to use lines to divide them into thought units. The children in looking them over should think in terms of pausing at the indicated "stop-lines." Here is a sample.

> The trees on the far-away hillsides / were billowing masses of crimson and gold.
> In the lonesome stretches of the long night / the watchers huddled together in fear.

As will be shown in the next section of the chapter, phrasing is related to those intonations which highlight the most important words in our speech and oral reading.

Emphasis and Intonations

Typically our voices use four levels or pitches. Most of our words are spoken at level 2; but when the key word in a phrase comes, the voice rises to level 3 to give it emphasis. In times of great stress or excitement, the voice may occasionally rise to level 4. In ending a statement of fact or in concluding an order, the voice fades away down to level 1 and into silence.

In the following sentences, the numbers above the syllables of the words indicate the inflections. Try reading them in the way indicated.

> 2 2 2 3 2 2   2   2 1
> I saw a ter-ri-ble storm com-ing.

> 2 2 2   2   2 3   2   2 3
> I did-n't think that you would do that.

> 3 2 2 2 4
> Oh, I see a ghost!

Good methods for making pupils aware of how their voices work in emphasizing key words through intonation, volume, and strategic pauses are to have them (1) listen to tape recordings of their natural conversation or discussion, (2) evaluate their oral reading of special exercises which call for strong emphasis on certain words, and (3) listen to commercial recordings of stories as told or read by experts. A particularly helpful exercise is the reading of the same sentence in several different ways according to shifts in the situations back of speech. For instance, have the italicized sentence read to bring out response to the following situations.

A young rabbit got into the garden and ate the lettuce.

1. Read the sentence as you normally would.
2. Make it clear that a rabbit, not a pony, got into the garden.
3. Show that it was a young, not old, rabbit.
4. Stress the place he got into—not a lawn, but a garden.
5. Make clear it was lettuce, not carrots, the rabbit ate.

In reading for point 2 above, the inflection of the voice would go up on the word *rabbit* to level 3, even 4; in point 3, on the word *young;* in point 5, on the word *lettuce.* Where would the stress be in point 4?

A similar exercise to be combined with a tape recording of the oral reading will contribute to an understanding of intonations. Have the following sentence read several times, with voice intonations distributed as follows:

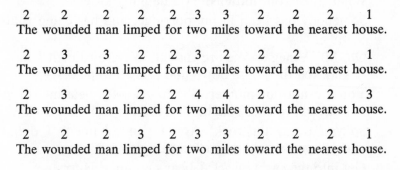

```
 2    2    2    2    2   3   3    2    2    2    1
The wounded man limped for two miles toward the nearest house.

 2    3    3    2    2   3   2    2    2    2    1
The wounded man limped for two miles toward the nearest house.

 2    3    2    2    2   4   4    2    2    2    3
The wounded man limped for two miles toward the nearest house.

 2    2    2    3    2   3   3    2    2    2    1
The wounded man limped for two miles toward the nearest house.
```

Next, have some exercises with intonations marked as in the foregoing and pauses for breath marked by widened spacing, as,

```
     2    2   2   3              3    2   2
 The blades of grass        heavy with dew

          3     2  2    2     1
     glistened in the morning sun.
```

Have the children notice that, in each group of words, at least one word is stressed by a rise in pitch, or a higher level of intonation. Emphasis gained through intonation is characteristic of spoken English. All longer sentences naturally break into major segments, each segment having at least one major word that is stressed by raising the level of intonation.

Turn back to the poem, "The Kite," in the early part of the chapter. Read it in such a way as to properly phrase and group the words and, within each word group, to stress the key word by using a higher pitch of voice. As you practice doing this, you are bound to be impressed by the extent of the help obtainable from punctuation in deciding the correct phrasing.

Probably the most effective and the easiest way to attain proper voice intonations in oral reading is to have the children frequently read lively dialogue in stories and verse. Select portions that reflect strong feeling. If the children have really put themselves into the situation depicted in the words, they are almost sure to stress the key words by changes in intonation. You may also make up sentences that are obviously heavily charged with emotion. Here are examples from literature and others of the authors' creation.

> What! Lost your mittens! You naughty kittens!
>
> Somebody has been in my porridge, and has eaten it all up!
>
> Oh, Mr. Vinegar! We are ruined! We are ruined! I have knocked the house down and it is all to pieces!
>
> You are not our mother. She has a soft, pleasant voice, but your voice is rough! You are the wolf!
>
> So you threw the rock! Aren't you ashamed? I didn't think you would do such a thing!
>
> Get into the car. Quick! A bear's coming! Hurry!

Subordination

Closely related to emphasizing important words by raising the pitch of the voice is the subordination of words and phrases that interrupt the main thought. These may be ejaculations or explanatory words. In the following excerpts, read the italicized parts in a voice much subdued so that the idea that has been interrupted may seem connected and almost continuous.

Godfrey Gordon Gustavus Gore—
No doubt you have heard the name before—
Was a boy who never would shut a door!

William Brighty Rands

One day (*to make the matter worse*),
    Before our names were fix'd,
As we were being wash'd by nurse,
    We got completely mix'd.
And thus, you see, by Fate's decree,
    (Or rather nurse's whim),
My brother John got christen'd me,
    And I got christen'd him.

Henry S. Leigh in "The Twins"

The gingham dog and the calico cat
Side by side on the table sat;
'Twas half-past twelve, and (*what do you think!*)
Nor one not t'other had slept a wink!
    The old Dutch clock and the Chinese plate
    Appeared to know as sure as fate
There was going to be a terrible spat.
    (I wasn't there; I simply state
    What was told to me by the Chinese plate!)

Eugene Field in "The Duel"

The skillful reader keeps the main thought going, and manages to insert the parenthetical phrases in a clear but subdued voice.

Continuity

Often sentences are long, and the effective oral reader keeps his voice suspended throughout so the listener will realize that the sentence is not yet ended—that the thought is continuing. In the reading of poetry in particular, the reader has to be careful not to drop his voice at the ends of lines where the thought continues to the next line. For instance, look back at lines 5, 6 and 7 of "The Duel" on page 13. You will see that these three lines form one meaningful word group and that no pause should follow the first two lines.

Sometimes continuity must be kept up over a series of lines. For instance in "Laughing Song" all the lines in the poem are leading toward the last two lines in the poem. Read it and see how the ideas keep building up and pointing toward the final lines.

LAUGHING SONG

When the green woods laugh with the voice of joy,
And the dimpling stream runs laughing by;
When the air does laugh with our merry wit,
And the green hill laughs with the noise of it;

When the meadows laugh with lively green,
And the grasshopper laughs in the merry scene;
When Mary and Susan and Emily
With their sweet round mouths sing, "Ha ha he!"

When the painted birds laugh in the shade,
When our table with cherries and nuts is spread;
Come live, and be merry, and join with me,
To sing the sweet chorus of "Ha ha he!"

William Blake

Integrated Application of the Skills

While each of the various skills has been presented separately in this section of the chapter, actually the oral reading of any bit of poetry or prose calls for the use of each of several skills in an integrated fashion. Try reading the following excerpts from the story, "The Sleeping Beauty," and note the need for using several of the skills at one and the same time.

The particular skills called for in this first excerpt are *enunciation, phrasing,* and *continuity.* Note how many of the words end in *d, t, st, ds,* and *k* sounds, all of which call for careful end-pronunciation. The reader must also keep continuously before his listeners the extended list of guests while still phrasing so as to catch a breath in a noninterruptive manner. (Note also the slanting lines that indicate the phrasing.)

> Not only did the king bid to the feast his kinfolk, friends, and acquaintances, / but also twelve fairy godmothers, / that they might bestow on the baby princess many gifts and favors.

In the following passage, the reader must use a faster *rate* to show the excitement and speed of action. At the same time, *intonations* may rise to level 4 (the highest) on some of the words; and the tone quality should reflect the angry resentment of the uninvited fairy.

> After the godmothers who had been invited had bestowed their gifts, / in rushed a thirteenth uninvited fairy. Aflame with anger and resentment, / she shrilled out: "The princess shall die! / In her fifteenth year she shall pierce a finger and fall dead!"

In contrast to the preceding passage, the following excerpt calls for a slower *rate* and no *intonation* higher than the third level. The voice quality will be that of composure, not excitement. There are many words whose endings must be spoken with *clarity* and *precision;* careful *phrasing* and *continuity* are called for as the complex picture of so many characters and objects ceasing to live or to move is presented. The clause following the word *queen* and the phrases which follow *cook* must be subordinated to the rest of the very long sentence.

> And all in the castle fell asleep; the king and queen, who had returned from their ride to the great hall, were deep in slumber, and with them their whole court. Even the dogs in the walled yard, the horses beside their mangers, the flies on every

wall, the pigeons perched on the roof, indeed the fire flicker-
ing on the hearth, were quiet in sleep; and the meat browning
on the spit grew cold, and the cook, about to pull the scullion's
locks for his careless mistakes, released him, and slept with the
rest.

The next two passages also have either a clause or a
phrase that should be *subordinated*. In both there are words
whose inverted order lends charm and style to the narrative;
but the reader has a great responsibility for maintaining *continuity* in ideas and highlighting the key ideas by *intonations*
that bring them to the fore in his listeners' minds.

> Over all the country spread rumor of the lovely sleeping
> Rosamond, for thus was the young princess named, and over
> the years many a king's son journeyed toward the palace and
> attempted to force a passage through the thorny hedge.

> Then the brave prince climbed up the steps and saw in the
> great hall all the court fast asleep, and above them, high on
> their golden thrones, slumbered thè king and his queen.

It is apparent that oral reading involves the use of many
skills which are learned only as the child receives training in
them. All during the school years in which such skills are being learned, he should be reading bits of the stories and poems
that he likes and wishes to present to his companions through
oral reading. Training alone is not enough; neither is trying
to read without any practice or needed skills. Experience
plus proper training spells success as an oral reader.

BIBLIOGRAPHY

DAWSON, MILDRED A. "The Role of Oral Reading in School and Life
Activities." *Elementary English,* January 1958, pp. 30-37.

EASTLAND, PATRICIA ANN. " 'Read-Aloud' Stories in the Primary Literature Program." *Reading Teacher,* December 1968, pp. 216-23.

LLOYD, D. "INTONATIONS AND READING." *Education* 85 (1964):
538-41.

ROBERTS, PAUL. *English Sentences,* pp. 167-79. New York: Harcourt,
1962.

———. *Patterns of English,* pp. 227-38; 275-76. New York: Harcourt,
1956.

ROBINSON, HELEN M. *Oral Aspects of Reading* (selected). Supplementary Reading Monographs, no. 82. Chicago: University of Chicago Press, 1955.

INTERNATIONAL READING ASSOCIATION. *Vistas in Reading* (selected). IRA Proceedings, vol. 12. Newark, Del.: International Reading Association, 1966:

—DEIGHTON, LEE C. "The Flow of Thought Through an English Sentence," pp. 322-26.

—GLIM, THEODORE E. "The Many Facets of Linguistics," pp. 318-22.

—O'DALY, ELIZABETH C. "Linguistics and the Teaching of Junior High School Reading," pp. 330-34.

—WHITEHEAD, ROBERT. "Oral Interpretation of Literature," pp. 84-87.

CHAPTER 2

How to Interpret Poetry Orally

Poetry is an intrinsic part of child life. Not only do children respond to the rhythm and melody of nursery rhymes and other simple poetry, but they frequently chant their own ideas in rhythmic, musical phrases. Note three-year-old Lauri who looked up at her uncle who was trudging along beside her in new-fallen snow. "Listen, Uncle Fred," she said. "I can say 'Jingle Bells' Lauri's way:

> Jingle bells, jingle bells,
>   See the snow come down.
> Jingle bells, jingle bells,
>   Santa Claus will come."

Almost any adult has heard a child chanting a refrain to the rhythmic action of jump rope, roller skates, swaying swing, tapping hammer, or even wind-blown rain beating on the window.

Too, children are prone to the use of figurative language. Their vivid ideas call for picturesque expressions, as for a boy who has let a baseball slip through his fingers. "Butterball!" or "Butterfingers!" greets his ears. A child out for a walk with Daddy will note an unusual church roof and say, "Look at that church's funny hat!" Or, seeing smoke suddenly billowing from a neighbor's chimney, a child will exclaim, "Wow! Ellis's fireplace must be smoking its biggest pipe!"

Poetry generally abounds in figurative language and, if its musical qualities are to be fully appreciated, must be read or spoken aloud for the enjoyment of both speaker and listener. This is especially true because the human voice—the child's in particular—is a sensitive musical instrument characterized by rhythm, melody, and tempo. Read the following rhymes silently, then orally. Note how oral rendition brings out the rhythm and melody.

> Peter, Peter, Pumpkin Eater,
> Had a wife and couldn't keep her.
> He put her in a pumpkin shell,
> And there he kept her very well.

> Mary, Mary, quite contrary,
>   How does your garden grow?
> Silver bells and cockle-shells,
>   And pretty maids in a row.

Since children's experiences with poetry begin early, many of them have known the delight of hearing jingles, nursery rhymes, and other poems read or recited by their parents long before they enter school. Nor have the catchy commercials of television escaped them. They enjoy repeating these jingles and rhymes over and over *ad nauseam* (as adults often see it) while at the same time they repeatedly ask to hear the longer, more intricate poems that have struck their fancy. For those children who have had happy experiences with good poetry, the task of the teacher is to continue and build on this pleasant past. For any who have lacked such experiences, teacher has the challenging job of filling the void.

The principal emphasis in this chapter is on the teacher's rendition of poetry, and much less attention is given to reading by children since the oral reading of poetry is an especially intricate job of stressing meanings more than rhythm, of maintaining continuity when lines end in mid-thought, of modulating the voice to suit delicate shifts in mood. The chapter ends with a listing of resource materials in the field of poetry.

The Teacher's Background in Poetry

If the teacher is to select and interpret poetry aptly, he must know much about children's interests and be familiar with the verse that is available and appealing. It is only as he chooses appropriate selections and properly presents them that the children will enjoy and appreciate the poetry they hear and later read for themselves.

Knowing Children's Preferences for Poetry

The teacher needs to be thoroughly acquainted with the facts of child development, especially with children's prevailing interests at the various stages of maturity. Inappropriate selection of poetry is a cardinal sin committed by many teachers and some publishers of textbooks, and the teacher must be able to select wisely what will most appeal to his pupils.

Generally speaking, children in the primary grades enjoy poems that contain repetitive phrases and unusual sounds. Nursery rhymes like the following are examples.

Higgledy, piggledy, my black hen,
She lays eggs for gentlemen;
Sometimes nine, sometimes ten,
Higgledy, piggledy, my black hen.

Intery, mintery, cutery corn,
Apple seed and apple thorn;
Wine, brier, limber lock,
Three geese in a flock,
One flew east, one flew west,
And one flew over the goose's nest.

Other typical favorites are William Brighty Rands' "Godfrey Gordon Gustavus Gore," "The Scissor-Man" by Madeleine Nightingale, "Old Ellen Sullivan" by Winifred Welles, and "Sh!" by James Tippett. Poetry for young girls and boys should reflect lively action and have themes centered about animals, other children, animate nature, fairies, and the world close at hand. So that the meaning can be grasped at the first hearing, poems should be simple, brief, and to the point. Even so, young children like a buildup of suspense and an element of surprise as in Walter de la Mare's "Someone," Marie Allen's "What Is It?" and the appealing old poem, "The Secret."

For older children poems of adventure, patriotism, humor, and mystery are appropriate. They accept with enthusiasm longer ballads and narrative poems with well-defined plots and real characters, such as John Greenleaf Whittier's "Barbara Frietchie," Alfred Noyes' "The Highwayman," and Henry Wadsworth Longfellow's "Paul Revere's Ride." Like their younger counterparts, these older girls and boys are resistant to vague poems that moralize and are replete with long, flowing descriptions and figures of speech.

Knowing Children's Poetry

Thorough familiarity with the world of children's poetry is a *must* for the teacher! The only way to be familiar is to read it often and in abundance. Only in this way can he know it well enough to be able to match up any one poem with the interest of his group or with a special occasion. It is imperative that a teacher keep at hand at least one good general anthology of poetry for children, this for browsing during spare time and for finding *the* poem that fits exactly a particular "teachable moment."

He should consistently leaf through current children's magazines and survey library shelves for the many fine specialized anthologies, picture books of verse, and the collected works of individual poets. A detailed list of such resources appears at the close of this chapter.

Knowing the Poets

The teacher who knows something of the life of the poet is himself likely to attain a greater understanding and appreciation of a poem's true meaning and thus be able to better communicate its sense and mood to his child listeners. It is truly difficult not to profit from knowing the great personal tragedies of Robert Louis Stevenson's life or the loss that prompted Eugene Field to write "Little Boy Blue."

A few minutes each week devoted to finding out about the poets will enable the teacher to know a great deal about most of the major ones. He can turn to the issues of the *Horn Book* and *Elementary English*, to the *Junior Book of Authors*,

Biographical Index, and certain anthologies which contain brief biographies of writers for children. The rewards for so doing are rich indeed in terms of the teacher's own enhanced enjoyment of poetry and the consequently greater enjoyment of it by his listeners.

Having a Fund of Favorite Poems

Every teacher should constantly add to his backlog of well-liked poems which he thoroughly enjoys reading to his pupils. These are the poems that will evoke his best efforts and, in turn, awaken enthusiasm in his listeners. Naturally the known interests of the children should be his prime criterion in selecting poems; but there are times when he should "let loose" and revel in sharing his particular loves in the realm of verse.

The teacher should, in addition, memorize certain favorites which he will have at his tongue-tip whenever they particularly fit in. In order to memorize, he need not sit down and devote long hours of precious time, since reading them aloud to the children from time to time will automatically result in memorization. Besides, there is nothing taxing about setting out to memorize a poem or two every few weeks. It is amazing how extensive an array of poetry can be mastered in this way.

Having and Using Requisite Skills in Presenting Poetry

A good poem is an artistic creation whose interpretation calls for perceptive, fluent performance. Poets often use unusual words, invert their sentences, and terminate an idea mid-line instead of at the end of the line. It is easy for a reader to be carried away by the metric beat of the words so that he wrongly pauses at the end of lines where a true interpretation of meaning calls for continuous reading past the line-ends into the opening words of the next line. In other words, the reading of poetry in a meaningful way is often no simple matter, and even the expert adult reader must prepare ahead of time if he is to do an adequate job. Most children can read well only those poems which are already familiar or which are so simply constructed that problems of word order and continuity do not arise. For the most part, the teacher should read the poems; children should listen.

It would be ideal if every teacher had taken courses in the oral interpretation of literature. Even if he has this background, he will have to take time to prepare ahead of time. Only thus can he determine the moods and ideas that the poet intended. In rehearsing, he should give attention primarily to conveying meanings, while making rhythm apparent. Tone quality should be consistent with the intended mood; voice intonations bring out the most significant words and subordinate less important ones. The teacher must be especially careful to maintain continuity whenever the wording carries a thought past the end of a line. It is apparent that a teacher needs to be expert in a galaxy of skills involved in interpreting poetry. These are discussed in the ensuing section of the chapter.

The Teacher's Presentation of Poetry

The teacher's role as an interpreter of poetry is an important one: How well children receive a poem and later present their own interpretation of it is determined largely by the quality of his presentation.

Reading poetry aloud *well* is an art which, like producing music, many teachers never master. Yet it is possible for every teacher who is willing to work hard at becoming an effective oral reader to learn to read verse aloud convincingly and entertainingly, even though not as professionally as a Charles Laughton or an Alexander Scourby.

Setting the Stage

The stage may already be set when some situation has arisen or an event is imminent that makes the reading of certain poetry highly appropriate. An approaching holiday, the coming of a circus, the first snow or a rainy day, some current event such as a new achievement in space, ongoing lessons in history or science—all these may set a natural stage for reading verse. One teacher successfully turns to the nursery rhyme "Blow, Wind, Blow" on a stormy day when the children are restless; or after a concentrated struggle with the multiplication combinations, she may have work briefly put aside while she recites Anna M. Pratt's "A Mortifying Mistake." On days when fatigue is apparent, she reads some such humorous poems as Ogden Nash's "The Tale of Custard the Dragon" or Beatrice Curtis Brown's "Jonathan Bing."

When a situation does not determine the timeliness of certain poems, the teacher must actively set the stage. She may hold a brief and pertinent discussion of an historical event, some current happening, or the imminent occurrence that will give the poem an appropriate setting. In case no such setting is available, the teacher may have to develop one. Mood music, a poignant story, an insightful cartoon, a bulletin board glowing with colorful pictures, or any of a multitude of approaches must be considered in selecting the right approach to the reading of a particular poem. (The approach may be as simple as the remark: "That airplane going over made me think of one of my favorite poems called 'High Flight.' Would you like to hear it?")

There should be an air of genuine anticipation whenever the teacher is about to present a poem. This may be aroused by the direction to clear the desks or to gather informally and quietly in a roomy corner of the classroom. Thus do the children get to recognize that something good is coming and that they are about to enjoy some of the teacher's favorite poems or share in some new ones he considers to have genuine appeal. Incidentally, that teacher who is long in his joy in sharing poetry but somewhat short in his reading abilities is likely to find that children respond warmly to his enthusiasm. As a result, he may grow in confidence and consequently in ability to bring out both meaning and beauty in his reading of verse.

The Teacher's Manner in Reciting Poetry

Above all, the teacher should be sincere, simple, direct. The poems are first in his mind. He is acting as an interpreter and, as such, stays in the background.

Even so, a genuine love of poetry and an enthusiasm for sharing it should permeate his manner. There is nothing more deadly in the oral interpretation of poetry than a matter-of-fact manner manifested by a monotone or a singsong that obscures meaning. To put it positively, the teacher-reciter must "do things with his voice" that will reflect moods and bring out salient ideas by its inflections. It must be so modulated that the poet himself seems to be interpreting the ideas and feelings.

Authorities differ about gestures as to whether they add or detract from a teacher's oral recitation of poetry. The use of gestures, it would seem, would be determined in part by his personality. If he consistently keeps himself in the background and lets his enthusiasm reflect itself naturally, he may or may not use gestures; but any gestures he does use should be spontaneous, though restrained, expressions of his inner reactions to poems. Any gestures that are forced and artificial will distract the children because their fascinated eyes will follow the gyrations which highlight the teacher-reciter, and take their minds from the meaning of the poetry.

A mild case of "hamming it up" may enthrall a group of small children, but at the same time leave them overexcited and oblivious of the poem's message. On the other hand, natural yet restrained gestures may be the very thing needed to arouse a lethargic group of junior high school pupils to the full meaning and impact of a poem. The best formulas are Know your poem; Know your audience; Know yourself; Keep your hands quiet unless their movements serve to enhance the pupils' interpretation and enjoyment of a poem.

Selecting Poems

Timeliness as determined by the ongoing curriculum and current events has already been discussed. Another consideration is the level of understanding and appreciation of which the child listeners are capable. The teacher must start where they are and take them from there. Just as tall buildings require deep foundations, the children must have had experiences with poetry over a period of time in order to develop deep roots. Whenever a teacher finds that his pupils have virtually no roots at all, having had little or no experience with poetry of fine quality, he may have to start behind the point at which he had chosen to begin.

Nursery rhymes make a good beginning for young children because of the marked rhythm, clear-cut rhymes, and liveliness in narrative. Older pupils may be attracted to poetry (which they may have decided they do not care for) by reading to them humorous verse, such as that represented by Lewis Carrolls' "Father William" or by an Edward Lear limerick like

> There was an old person whose habits
> Induced him to feed upon rabbits;
>   When he'd eaten eighteen,
>   He turned perfectly green,
> Upon which he relinquished those habits.

For the reluctant dragons who manifest an indifference or even dislike for poetry, humorous verse may prove to be the one key to the poetry kingdom. This is particularly true of boys who tend to be wary of poetry of any kind; but humorous poems may be able to slip into their lives through the back door. They are likely to find it difficult to put down such books as A. A. Milne's *The World of Christopher Robin,* John Ciardi's *The Reason for the Pelican,* Laura E. Richards' *Tirra Lirra,* and William Cole's anthology, *Humorous Poetry for Children,* once the teacher brings these books to their attention by reading selected bits aloud.

Conveying Meaning

One teacher who is frequently invited to talk with children about the meaning and fun of poetry begins by reciting the following lines from Chaucer's *Canterbury Tales*:

> Whan that Aprille with his shoures sote
> The droghte of March hath perced to the rote,
> And bathed every vein in swich licour,
> Of which vertu engendred is the flour; . . .
> And specially, from every shires ende
> Of Engelond, to Caunterbury they wende,
> The holy blisful martir for to seke,
> That hem hath holpen, whan that they were seke.

Children of all ages are invariably delighted with her recital. As they put it, they like the "funny, mysterious, not-American" words. Then the visiting teacher asks if there is anyone who did not like the poem and if he can tell why. There is always at least one brave child who, having been pre-warned about being polite to guests, nevertheless timidly raises his hand and quietly says, "I didn't like it because I didn't understand it."

"Exactly right, boys and girls," says the visitor. "Poetry must be fully understood to be *really* enjoyed. For, without knowing the meaning of the words and the ideas that the poet wished to give us, the poem *is* just a mouthful of 'funny' words as you called them."

The point of this is that in preparing to present a poem, the reader must first think through the meaning to be conveyed. It is his task to lift the idea of the poem from the printed page and transport it to the minds of his listeners. This is not an easy task. To do the job well, he must adjust the volume of his voice and modulate his tone quality, determine proper phrasing and stress, and study out the continuity, essential if meanings and moods are to be effectively interpreted. This is not to say that only one "pattern" of oral interpretation is possible. As a matter of fact, various interpretations are desirable. Just as the concertmaster's individual interpretation of a musical score increases our appreciation of it, so does a reader's individual interpretation of a bit of poetry bring new nuances of meaning to listeners. To illustrate the point, each stanza of James Whitcomb Riley's "Little Orphant Annie" closes much like this:

> An' the Gobble-uns 'll git *you*
> Ef you
>   Don't
>   Watch
>   Out!

Most child-listeners do not react strongly to these lines if the reading is even in rate and tone of voice. However if the reader slows the pace of the poem just before enunciating these two lines, then accents "Gobble-uns" and explodes on "git you," listening becomes active. The children feel personally involved with the goblin that threatens to get them.

Such an interpretation of "Little Orphant Annie" cannot, however, precede the knowledge of what Riley *meant* to happen or of the meaning he *intended* the lines to convey. So while a reader is permitted to "put meaning into" a poem, he must first learn to "get meaning out of" it.

There follow some major suggestions for conveying meaning.

1. A poem should be presented only if it is within the children's intellectual grasp and interest range. Intellectually, the pupils must be able to cope with the vocabulary and its context of meanings. The theme of the poem must be understandable and of at least potential interest.

2. In preparing to present the poem, the teacher should read it aloud to himself. By so doing he can determine its general rhythm and rhyme scheme, note which words are most important and should be stressed, and find any words and place names that will probably be unfamiliar, and which should be written on the board for discussion before the poem is presented. (Sometimes when the general meanings and theme will be apparent despite difficult words, the teacher may prefer to do such board work after reading it to the pupils so that the child-listeners will have had the benefit of interpreting the words through the more meaningful context.)

Putting important new words and phrases on the board for examination and discussion is a vital part of the "gaining meaning" process. Most poems, even the briefest Mother Goose rhymes, have their difficult words or phrases which need clarification. For example, note the italicized words in this rhyme:

Ride a *cock horse* to *Banbury Cross*
To see a fine lady upon a white horse;
Rings on her fingers and *bells on her toes,*
She shall have music wherever she goes.

Lacking an explanatory picture of the rhyme, children will have little chance of knowing what a "cock horse" is unless the teacher explains that it is a rocking horse. "Banbury Cross" and "bells on her toes" merit similar explanation if the rhyme is to have meaning, and not be a mere assembly of rhythm and rhyme.

After meanings have been cleared up, the poem should be read again so that meaning and rhyme and rhythm can merge smoothly in the pleasant experience of listening and forming mental images.

3. From this point on, the children's understanding may be deepened by a summation of the entire poem in a sentence or two. Note, for example, the discussion that followed the reading of this poem.

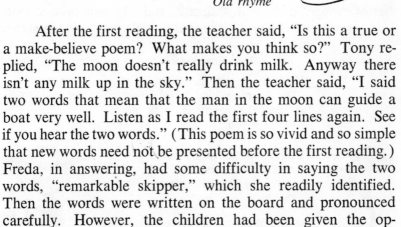

THE MAN IN THE MOON

The Man in the Moon as he sails the sky
 Is a very remarkable skipper,
But he made a mistake when he tried to take
 A drink of milk from the Dipper.

He dipped right out of the Milky Way,
 And slowly and carefully filled it,
The Big Bear growled, and the Little Bear howled
 And frightened him so that he spilled it.

Old rhyme

After the first reading, the teacher said, "Is this a true or a make-believe poem? What makes you think so?" Tony replied, "The moon doesn't really drink milk. Anyway there isn't any milk up in the sky." Then the teacher said, "I said two words that mean that the man in the moon can guide a boat very well. Listen as I read the first four lines again. See if you hear the two words." (This poem is so vivid and so simple that new words need not be presented before the first reading.) Freda, in answering, had some difficulty in saying the two words, "remarkable skipper," which she readily identified. Then the words were written on the board and pronounced carefully. However, the children had been given the opportunity of using contextual clues in recognizing meanings.

4. Further meaning and enrichment may grow out of discussing the experiences the children have had in relation to

the concepts back of the poem. In connection with "The Man in the Moon," they might discuss the location and shape of the Big Dipper and the facelike appearance of the full moon. Another possibility is the comparison of the poem with a similar one, such as Vachel Lindsay's "The Moon's the North Wind's Cooky."

Through all of this, though, the teacher must keep in mind that analysis that is too detailed is likely to kill children's interest in a poem. He must make sure that the child is helped to arrive at a meaningful interpretation in the quickest, most enjoyable way possible.

Using the Skills That Contribute to Understanding

Many adult readers are weak in their oral interpretation of poetry so far as their phrasing is concerned. They tend to surrender themselves too completely to the rhythm of the poem and not to group the words in terms of their close relationships. The skill of properly grouping words into phrases based on related thought units is difficult to master. This fact is made apparent when the following poem is considered in terms of three phrasing problems: (1) a sentence with a single complete thought as in lines 3 and 4; (2) a sentence with a number of thought units as in stanza 2; and (3) punctuation stops and/or run-on lines and/or parenthetical remarks as in stanza 3.

THE FERRYMAN

"Ferry me across the water,
  Do, boatman, do."
"If you've a penny in your purse
  I'll ferry you."

"I have a penny in my purse,
  And my eyes are blue;
So ferry me across the water,
  Do, boatman, do."

"Step into my ferry-boat,
  Be they black or blue,
And for the penny in your purse
  I'll ferry you."

Christina Rossetti

Broadly speaking, the problems of *phrasing* are solved if the reader has fully recognized and interpreted the meaning of the sentences, whether rhythmic and rhyming or not. For instance, the reader will have noticed that the first stanza in "The Ferryman" represents the speech of two persons—a young lady and a boatman. He must then pass this awareness on to his listeners by a change in the pitch of his voice as he moves from line 2 to line 3.

It is easy, too, for the oral reader to *stress* the wrong words as he interprets a poem. It has been said that nouns, verbs, adjectives, and adverbs should receive the greatest stress. It is sure that unimportant words like the articles (*a, an, the*), prepositions, and conjunctions rarely are stressed. The basic meaning of the words in a sentence really determines the stress, especially when there are contrasting ideas as in Elizabeth Coatsworth's *swift* things and *slow* things or Laura E. Richards' three little monkeys that swing *high* and *low*. In cases of contrast, it is often the adjectives or adverbs that express differences and should receive the strongest stress.

Poetry brings many problems of *continuity,* especially with lines that run on into the next line and should be read without a pause at the end of the line. The following Mother Goose rhyme illustrates how necessary it is to keep the voice suspended at the end of lines where the thought is not yet complete, how there should be no pause in the midst of phrases that belong together. In this poem there should be continuity at the end of lines 1, 3, 5, and 7; the good reader does not surrender to the rhythm and let the beat of the words induce pauses that break thought.

> Cocks crow in the morn
>   To tell us to rise,
> And he who lies late
>   Will never be wise.
>
> For early to bed
>   And early to rise,
> Is the way to be healthy
>   And wealthy and wise.

Problems of *subordination* also confront the reader of poetry. When side remarks are inserted, the teacher must be sure to lower the voice so that the major ideas are made important and the insertions subordinated. Note the parenthetical phrases in this stanza from Henry Sambrooke Leigh's "The Twins."

> One day (to make the matter worse),
>   Before our names were fix'd,
> As we were being wash'd by nurse,
>   We got completely mix'd.
> And thus, you see, by Fate's decree,
>   (Or rather nurse's whim),
> My brother John got christen'd *me*,
>   And I got christen'd *him*.

The two parenthetical phrases are not the only ones to be subordinated. "You see" in the fifth line is also an insertion. The poem also illustrates the fact that italicized words should usually be strongly stressed.

Reacting to the Music of Poetry

Poetry is characterized by rhythm—usually with a regular beat—rhyming words, words whose sounds reflect the mood the poet is trying to portray, alliteration, and other musical effects. While meaning should be put foremost, the reader should still react to the flow of the rhythm, the melody of the words, and the quickness of short words with short-vowel sounds and the lingering effect of longer words that feature long vowels. Words skip or march or drag their feet in response to the mood that they express; and the reader should use their sounds to reinforce his interpretation of meaning.

The following Mother Goose rhyme illustrates the use of words that flow from a light heart and that skip in merry measure. As the teacher recites the rhyme she will mark the

Hickory, Dickory, dock!
The mouse ran up the clock;
The clock struck one,
And down he run.
Hickory, Dickory, dock!

beat (') by slapping two fingers of one hand into the palm of the other, by tapping lightly on a desk or book, or by finger-tipping. After one or two such recitations, the children are invited to join in the rhythmic action as the teacher again recites the rhyme. (With more advanced and highly rhythmic poems, older pupils prefer to clap lightly or snap their fingers.)

The rhythmic beat of "Hickory, Dickory" almost calls for children to skip as the rhyme is recited. In the beginning, one boy and one girl may be asked to skip while the entire class speaks the rhyme together. More mature pupils may work up sound effects to fit a poem; for instance, the galloping of a horse or zooming of an airplane. Some poems lend themselves to rhythmic pantomime, to marching, or to dancing as a suitable poem is repeated. "Grand Old Duke of York" almost demands that pupils march to its steady beat.

There is no end to the list of poems which are suited to rhythmic interpretation. The Mother Goose rhymes are an excellent source of materials for primary children because of their simple, tuneful words. Older pupils prefer poems of greater depth and greater variety in pitch, voice volume and quality, and rate. The following chart lists a few poems and the corresponding rhythmic movements.

POEM	RHYTHMIC MOVEMENT	LEVEL
Pease Porridge Hot (old rhyme)	Clapping	Primary
Pat-a-cake (Mother Goose)	Clapping	Primary
Hickory Dickory Dock (Mother Goose)	Ticking clock	Primary
A Cat Came Fiddling (Mother Goose)	Dancing	Primary
Pop Goes the Weasel (old rhyme)	Dancing	Primary
Dance to Your Daddie (Mother Goose)	Dancing	Primary
Rap-a-tap-tap (Mother Goose)	Hammering	Primary
Hippity Hop (old rhyme)	Hopping	Primary
Jump–Jump–Jump (Kate Greenaway)	Jumping	Primary
Grand Old Duke of York (old rhyme)	Marching	Primary
Bell Horses (old rhyme)	Prancing	Primary
The Horsemen (Walter de la Mare)	Prancing	Primary
Ride Away, Ride Away (Mother Goose)	Prancing	Primary

POEM	RHYTHMIC MOVEMENT	LEVEL
The Huntsmen (Walter de la Mare)	Running	Primary
Follow My Bangalorey Man (Mother Goose)	Running	Primary
To Market, to Market (Mother Goose)	Skipping	Primary
Soft Step (Georgette Agnew)	Walking	Primary
Diddle Diddle Dumpling (Mother Goose)	Walking	Primary
Hot Cross Buns (Mother Goose)	Walking	Primary
Ride a Cock Horse (Mother Goose)	Trotting	Primary
The Shiny Little House (Nancy Hayes)	Ticking clock	Intermediate
How They Brought the Good News From Ghent to Aix	Galloping sounds	Intermediate
A Sea-Song from the Shore (James W. Riley)	Humming sound	Intermediate
The Baby Goes to Boston (Laura E. Richards)	Jiggling (as a locomotive)	Intermediate
Jump or Jiggle (Evelyn Beyer)	Jiggling	Intermediate
The Wind (Robert Louis Stevenson)	Swinging arms	Intermediate
The Swing (Robert Louis Stevenson)	Swinging arms	Intermediate
Feet (Irene Thompson)	Walking	Intermediate
The Swing (Mary Osborn)	Swinging arms	Intermediate
Choosing Shoes (Ffrida Wolfe)	Light tripping	Intermediate
Gallop Away (unknown)	Trotting	Intermediate
Aeroplane (Mary McB. Green)	Zooming sound	Intermediate

Helping Children to Interpret Poetry Orally

There are two primary goals in teaching children to interpret poetry orally. The first is to awaken within them the power to understand the poetry which they are to read aloud. The second is to develop their skills of delivery so that they present poems effectively.

Gaining Meaning from Poetry

As has already been demonstrated, children usually should read aloud only those poems with which they are relatively familiar or which are decidedly simple in context and structure. In the case of the former, the teacher has the responsibility for making sure that a poem is meaningful. To recapitulate briefly, the teacher does the following:

1. He sets the stage by discussing related previous experiences, posting colorful pictures, telling a story, or otherwise bringing the poem's topic and theme to the fore before the verse is presented.
2. He raises some question for the pupils to keep in mind as they listen, this question being designed to bring out the salient idea.
3. In case the poem's contextual clues do not clearly bring out the meaning of heretofore unfamiliar key words, he calls attention to unusual and unfamiliar words whose meaning is basic to understanding the poem.
4. He presents the poem as effectively as possible through modulating his voice, stressing main ideas, phrasing properly and, in general, reflecting as authentically and impressively as he can the poet's intended mood and meaning.

After so meaningful a presentation—often several readings being desirable—the children should be able to present the poem in a truly interpretative manner, the skills of delivery guaranteed by their understanding of the poem and their aptness for imitating the teacher's way of presenting the poem. After considerable experience in reading or reciting these familiar poems, they should be ready to study and develop for themselves effective ways of delivering simple, unfamiliar poems.

Learning the Skills of Delivery

In general, children will *phrase* quite well those poems which they really understand. They will, however, need to rehearse carefully before reading and so make sure of smooth fluency as well as good phrasing. For boys and girls who need specific practice in handling problems of phrasing, the following procedures may prove useful:

1. The teacher may read a poem in which he groups thought units or phrases incorrectly. This fact may be made more apparent by writing some lines on the and indicating the wrong phrasing by double vertical lines; for instance,

> I have a penny // in my purse //
> And my eyes // are blue //
> So ferry me // across the water
> Do, // boatman, do.

The pupils readily note the choppiness and broken thoughts in so faulty a division of lines.

2. If a child reader continues to have difficulty with *phrasing* and proper *continuity*, the teacher should put the proper division of the lines on the board. Note the original placement of lines in this stanza, then the rearrangement to encourage meaningful reading.

Summer is nigh!
How do I know?
  Why, this very day
A robin sat
  On a tilting spray,
And merrily sang
  A song of May.
Jack Frost has fled
  From the rippling brook;

And a trout peeped out
  From his shady nook.
A butterfly too
  Flew lazily by,
And the willow catkins
  Shook from on high
Their yellow dust
  As I passed by:
And so I know
  That summer is nigh.

Unknown

> This very day a robin sat on a tilting spray //
> And merrily sang a song of May //
> Jack Frost has fled from the rippling brook //
> And a trout peeped out from his shady nook //
> A butterfly too flew lazily by //
> And the willow catkins // (*too long a phrase for one breath*)
>   shook from on high their yellow dust (*shook not separated from dust*)

3. The teacher can duplicate copies of poems. He and the children together can discuss and determine the correct phrasing which will yield meaningful results. This can also be done at the chalkboard as a class exercise.

Another feature of effective reading of poetry is *stress*. Nonfluent readers often progress word by word, in monotone, so that listeners are likely to miss most of the meaning and all of the mood that the poet has intended. A first-grade child, for instance, may read the first line in the old Mother Goose rhyme in broken rhythm and uneven emphasis while struggling with unfamiliar words, there being long pauses before difficult words and undue emphasis whenever one such hard word is recognized and spoken. The line would then be read as follows:

Three little   MICE   sat down to   SPIN

Listeners would indeed have difficulty in getting the sense of what has been read, especially since the voice is likely to be a monotone on all the familiar words. It is important that children be familiar with the poem to be read, that they be well acquainted with its theme and wording, and that they sense the mood to be portrayed. Even so, the teacher should probably raise some questions that will bring to the forefront the main ideas, to make sure that the really crucial words will be stressed.

One activity which will highlight the importance of proper stress on critical words is playing the "interpretation game." A phrase or sentence from a poem may be written on the board several times so that a different word can be underlined each time. The trick is to read the excerpt with emphasis on the underlined word (here shown by italics).

I'll ferry you.   (I, and no one else will do it.)
I'll *ferry* you.   (We'll go by boat, not train or car.)
I'll ferry *you*.   (You, and no one else, will I take.)

The volume and quality of the *voice* are other matters of concern. The teacher's task is to help the children develop pleasing, well-modulated, audible voices. The soft-spoken, in particular, should reach the stage of automatically considering the persons sitting farthest away, and make sure their voices are perfectly audible to the most distant listeners. All should realize that the expression of caution calls for a very subdued tone, whereas great excitement is characterized by a piping tone. Interpretation in general requires a voice bespeaking the feeling to be portrayed. Stories like "The Three Billy Goats Gruff" or "The Three Bears" call for variations in pitch from light to very gruff tones.

Enunciation is a rather common problem that needs attention. The children may run words together as "gonna" for "going to" or "wanna" for "want to." The words ending in the sounds of *d, t, b, p, t,* and *k* may need special practice. The teacher may use rhymes that feature such sounds (Jack Sprat or Little Miss Muffet, for example) and have them read aloud, with particular effort to say the critical word-endings clearly, or may make up sentences like these to be read aloud.

Frank shook Mike's stick at the snake.

Fred said Ned should shed his coat.

Bert thought Kip would flip at the slick trick we played.

The *rhythm* in poetry constitutes much of its beauty, and children may need help in bringing it out without lapsing into singsong effects. There are some activities that may help to highlight rhythm in a constructive way.

1. Having young children listen to and work with the various rhythm-making instruments helps to sharpen their awareness of rhythm in poetry. In lieu of lengthy discussions, it is well to substitute the playing of triangles, drums, and cymbals very softly in response to the meter of rhymes the teacher is repeating or that the children are speaking in unison.

2. Writing free verse also may help. This may take the form of Haiku, a form of Japanese poetry consisting

of three unrhymed, unmetered lines expressing a moment of insight. The first line of a Haiku poem contains five syllables, the second line seven, and the third line five; for example,

The snow comes drifting
as angels shake their pillows
high up in heaven.

3.   The teacher should expose the children to a variety of jingles and verses that suggest rhythmic movements such as clapping, hopping, skipping, dancing, and marching. Here not only rhythm but fast and slow tempo, high and low pitch, soft and loud voices can be featured.

Rate of reading is still another element to be considered in presenting poetry. The teacher can demonstrate the importance of using an appropriate rate by reading contrasting poems such as "Wee Willie Winkie" and Walter de la Mare's "Tired Tim," the first briskly to indicate the lad's running, the latter in an almost drowsy manner. He may even conclude the latter presentation with a wide yawn. If the point has not gotten across, either poem may be read in the completely opposite way so as to demonstrate how an inappropriate rate spoils the mood and intrinsic meaning of each bit of verse.

To demonstrate further the effect of rate on interpretation, he can have the pupils prepare to read fluently other poems in both slow- and quick-paced fashion. For example, they cannot help but note how the spirit of the following poem is lost when it is read in a slow and dragging tempo.

THE CHILD AND THE FAIRIES

The woods are full of fairies!
  The trees are all alive;
The river overflows with them,
  See how they dip and dive!
What funny little fellows!
  What dainty little dears!
They dance and peep, and prance and leap,
  And utter fairy cheers.

I'd like to tame a fairy,
  To keep it on a shelf,
To see it wash its little face
  And dress its little self.
I'd teach it pretty manners,
  It always would say, "Please";
And then, you know, I'd make it sew
  And curtsey with its knees.

Unknown

It will be obvious that a poem filled with such light and airy words as "dainty" and "peep" should be read lightly and rather quickly.

In helping children to focus upon problems of rate and timing as they read poetry aloud, the teacher should bring out these points:

1. Read the way you talk!
2. Think about what you are reading!
   Remember, if there is excitement or airiness or titillating mystery in the lines of the theme of a poem, the reader will naturally increase his speed of oral reading. If there is real depth of meaning, he will slow down to permit the listener to follow the thought.
3. Read more slowly than you think you should!
   Most children, in their desire to complete the reading of a poem, read much too fast. Consequently enunciation suffers because they fail to give the vowels and consonants their full values.

Enjoying Rhyming Effects

Necessary to real appreciation of poetry is a deepening understanding of the significance of rhyme. For all too many children, rhyme along with lively meter is all that poetry is or ever will be. It is necessary for them to learn that poetry is much more than lines ending in words that sound alike. Rather, it involves the way in which vowels and consonants are strung together in patterns of sound, beautiful in the deep resonance of nasals and singing of certain consonants. Here are some suggestions for developing children's appreciation of rhymes.

1. The teacher reads simple poems with clearly apparent rhymes. He will then read the poems again, this time pausing at the end of each line so that the children can supply the rhyming word. Young children genuinely enjoy this type of experience.

2. A variation on the foregoing procedure will appeal to middle graders. Let a small group of fluent readers prepare to read a poem. They will then read the poem as a whole, before the class, later repeat it as the remainder of the class supply the rhyming words which the pupil readers have intentionally omitted. Another possibility is to have the class raise hands as soon as a rhyming word is heard, or all may repeat the rhyming words softly as these occur.

3. The teacher may write short, rhyming poems on the board and underline the rhyming words. Sometimes there should be internal rhymes to be marked as in these lines from "The Little Dutch Garden."

Tulips and *roses* and little pink *posies*— . . . .
'Mid 'wildering *mazes* of spinach and *daisies,* . . . .

Pupils as Readers and as Listeners

The business of reading poetry is a two-way street. Both the child reader and his listeners gain from the experience of interpreting poems orally. So as to make certain that both the communicator and the receptor profit, the teacher should remember the following:

1. Be sure that the reader has the only copy of the poem which is being read. If other copies are available, they should be put aside.
2. Direct the listeners' attention to what is being read, not to the reader.
3. Have each child prepare to read a different poem to the class. A child gives his best effort if he chooses what he himself enjoys and wants to share, especially if he knows that he has exclusive rights to the reading of that particular poem and if he is sure that it is new to his listeners.
4. Do not require every child to read aloud, and never rush any child into this kind of activity. Many shy children will have their small cups of confidence drained by an unfortunate experience into which they have been pushed. However, do call on any backward child as soon as he manifests an interest in reading or reciting a poem.

Providing Variety in Approach

There is no *one best way* to teach the oral interpretation of poetry. Whereas one child may be completely comfortable in standing before his group and reading aloud, another may shrink from doing it. The teacher should encourage children to think up their own techniques of presentation, especially in the case of the more able. Among the possible techniques are the following:

1. Dramatizing and pantomiming poetry: One child may read a poem while one or more other children may act it out. Such poems as Elizabeth Madox Roberts' "Mumps," Dorothy Aldis' "Setting the Table," Florence Jaques' "A Goblinade," Beatrice Brown's "Jonathan Bing," and Rachel Field's "The Ice Cream Man" are good starters.

2. Reading poetry to music: Here appropriate background music on a recording or a tape is played as the poem is recited. The poems of A. A. Milne and Rudyard Kipling are especially adaptable for this type of activity.

3. Reading and recording original poems: Whether as free verse or in traditional metrical, rhymed lines, many children enjoy writing and then reading to the class their own original products. Limericks are good for use in the higher grades. For later use, these poems can be typed and lettered and posted on the bulletin board, mounted in scrap books, or put on charts. Original music or tape-recorded selections can be played as accompaniment to these later presentations.

Resources

The following list of resources is arranged in four groups. The first two sections offer an arrangement of selected books of poetry and verse published since 1965 for younger children and for older students. The third section lists more recently published professional books concerned in part or in whole with the methodologies of teaching poetry. A list of recent, representative records (R) and tapes (T), with a directory of distributors following, closes the chapter.

Books of Poetry for Younger Children

AIKEN, CONRAD. *Cats and Bats and Things With Wings.* New York: Atheneum, 1965.

ARNDT, URSULA. *All the Silver Pennies.* New York: Macmillan, 1967.

BELTING, NATALIA. *Calendar Moon.* New York: Holt, Rinehart & Winston, 1966.

BISHOP, ANN. *Riddle Raddle, Fiddle Faddle.* Racine, Wis.: Whitman Pub., 1966.

COLE, WILLIAM. *Oh. What Nonsense!* New York: Viking Pr., 1966.

DE FOREST, CHARLOTTE. *The Prancing Pony: Nursery Rhymes from Japan.* New York: Walker & Co., 1968.

DE REGNIERS, BEATRICE. *Circus.* New York: Viking Pr., 1966.

FISHER, AILEEN. *In the Woods, In the Meadow, In the Sky.* New York: Scribner, 1965.

FLANDERS, MICHAEL. *Creatures Great and Small.* New York: Holt, Rinehart & Winston, 1965.

FRANK, JOSETTE. *More Poems to Read to the Very Young.* New York: Random, 1968.

LARRICK, NANCY. *Piper, Pipe That Song Again: Poems for Boys and Girls.* New York: Random, 1965.

LENT, BLAIR. *From King Boggen's Hall to Nothing-At-All: A Collection of Improbable Houses and Unusual Places Found in Traditional Rhymes and Limericks.* Boston: Little, Brown, 1967.

LEWIS, RICHARD. *In a Spring Garden.* New York: Dial, 1965.

LIVINGSTON, MYRA. *The Moon and a Star and Other Poems.* New York: Harcourt, Brace & World, 1965.

MACBETH, GEORGE. *Noah's Journey.* New York: Viking Pr., 1966.

MAMLOCK, GWYNETH. *Magic Carpet to Animal Rhyme Land.* Irvington-on-Hudson, N. Y.: Harvey, 1966.

MARGOLIS, RICHARD. *Only the Moon and Me.* Philadelphia: Lippincott, 1969.

McCORD, DAVID. *All Day Long.* Boston: Little, Brown, 1966.

McFERRAN, ANN. *Poems to be Read Aloud.* Camden, N. J.: Nelson, 1965.

McGINLEY, PHYLLIS. *Wonderful Time.* Philadelphia: Lippincott, 1966.

MIZUMURA, KAZUE. *I See the Winds.* New York: Crowell, 1966.

MOORE, LILLIAN. *I Feel the Same Way.* New York: Atheneum, 1967.

O'NEILL, MARY. *Take a Number.* New York: Doubleday, 1968.

O'NEILL, MARY. *What Is That Sound!* New York: Atheneum, 1966.

PRELUTSKY, JACK. *A Gopher in the Garden and Other Poems.* New York: Macmillan, 1967.

ROCKWELL, THOMAS. *Rackety-Bang.* New York: Pantheon, 1969.

SMARIDGE, NORAH. *Scary Things.* Nashville: Abingdon, 1969.

SNYDER, ZILPHA. *Today Is Saturday.* New York: Atheneum, 1969.

STOUTENBURG, ADRIEN. *The Crocodile's Mouth.* New York: Viking Pr., 1969.

Books of Poetry for Older Students

ADOFF, ARNOLD. *I Am the Darker Brother: An Anthology of Modern Poems by Negro Americans.* New York: Macmillan, 1968.

BARNSTONE, ALIKI. *The Real Tin Flower: Poems About the World At Nine.* New York: T. Y. Crowell, 1968.

BONTEMPS, ARNA. *Hold Fast To Dreams.* Chicago: Follett, 1969.

CAUDILL, REBECCA. *Come Along!* New York: Holt, Rinehart & Winston, 1969.

CAUSLEY, CRARLES. *Modern Ballads and Story Poems.* New York: Watts, 1965.

COATSWORTH, ELIZABETH. *The Sparrow Bush.* New York: Norton, 1966.

COLE, WILLIAM. *A Book of Nature Poems.* New York: Viking Pr., 1969.

DUNNING, STEPHEN. *Reflections on a Gift of Watermelon Pickle.* New York: Lothrop, 1966.

DUNNING, STEPHEN. *Some Haystacks Don't Even Have Any Needle and Other Complete Modern Poems.* New York: Nothrop, 1969.

GREGORY, HORACE. *The Silver Swan: Poems of Romance and Mystery.* New York: Holt, Rinehart & Winston, 1969.

GROSS, SARAH. *Every Child's Book of Verse.* New York: Watts, 1968.

HANNUM, SARA. *Lean Out the Window.* New York: Atheneum, 1965.

LARRICK, NANCY. *On City Streets: An Anthology of Poetry.* Philadelphia. Lippincott, 1968.

LEWIS, CLAUDIA. *Poems of Earth and Space.* New York: Dutton, 1967.

LEWIS, RICHARD. *Miracles: Poems by Children of the English-Speaking World.* New York: Simon and Schuster, 1966.

LEWIS, RICHARD. *Out of the Earth I Sing: Poetry and Songs of Primitive Peoples of the World.* New York: Norton, 1968.

LIVINGSTON, MYRA. *A Crazy Flight and Other Poems.* New York: Harcourt, Brace & World, 1969.

LIVINGSTON, MYRA. *A Tune Beyond Us: A Collection of Poetry.* New York: Harcourt, Brace & World, 1968.

LOWENFELS, WALTER. *The Writing on the Wall: 108 American Poems of Protest.* New York: Doubleday, 1969.

MERRIAM, EVE. *Independent Voices.* New York: Atheneum, 1968.

MORRISON, LILLIAN. *Sprints and Distances: Sports in Poetry and Poetry in Sport.* New York: T. Y. Crowell, 1965.

O'NEILL, MARY. *Words Words Words.* New York: Doubleday, 1966.

STARBIRD, KAYE. *A Snail's a Failure Socially.* Philadelphia: Lippincott, 1966.

SWENSON, MAY. *Poems to Solve.* New York: Scribner, 1966.

Professional Books on Methodologies of Teaching Poetry

A Curriculum for English: Poetry for the Elementary Grades. Lincoln, Nebraska: U. of Nebr. Pr., 1966.

APPLEGATE, MAUREE. *When the Teacher Says, "Write a Poem."* Evanston, Ill.: Harper & Row, 1965.

ARBUTHNOT, MAY HILL. *Children and Books.* 3d ed. Glenview, Ill.: Scott, Foresman, 1964.

ARNSTEIN, FLORA. *Poetry in the Elementary Classroom.* New York: Appleton, 1962.

DUNNING, STEPHEN. *Teaching Literature to Adolescents: Poetry.* Glenview, Ill.: Scott, Foresman, 1966.

GEORGIOU, CONSTANTINE. *Children and Their Literature.* Englewood Cliffs, N. J.: Prentice-Hall, Inc., 1969.

HOLLOWELL, LILLIAN. *A Book of Children's Literature.* 3d ed. New York: Holt, Rinehart & Winston, 1966.

HUBER, MIRIAM BLANTON. *Story and Verse for Children.* 3d ed. New York: Macmillan, 1967.

HUCK, CHARLOTTE, and YOUNG, DORIS. *Children's Literature in the Elementary School.* 2d ed. New York: Holt, Rinehart & Winston, 1968.

RASMUSSEN, CARRIE. *Speech Methods in the Elementary Schools.* New York: Ronald, 1962.

WALTER, NINA WILLIS. *Let Them Write Poetry.* New York: Holt, Rinehart & Winston, 1962.

WHITEHEAD, ROBERT. *Children's Literature: Strategies of Teaching.* Englewood Cliffs, N. J.: Prentice-Hall, Inc., 1968.

Records (R) and Tapes (T)

R   "Black Boy." Read by Brock Peters. Gr 7-12. Caedmon Records.

R   "Bread and Jam for Frances." Read by Anita Clever. Gr K-3. Columbia Records.

T   Caedmon Literature Tape Reels Series. Gr 1-12. Ten items in the series, ranging from *Aesop's Fables* to *The Poetry of Langston Hughes.* Caedmon Records.

T   Caedmon Literature Tape Cassettes Series. Gr 1-12. Ten items in the series, ranging from *Alice in Wonderland* to *Life on the Mississippi.* Caedmon Records.

R   "Carol Channing Reads and Sings." Gr 1-6. Houghton Mifflin.

T   Children's Classics on Tape. Gr K-8. Thirty-three items in the series. Bloch.

R   "Great Negro Americans." Read by Hilda Simms and Frederick O'Neal. Gr 4-12. Alan Sands Productions.

R   "Happy Birthday to You! And Other Stories." Read by Hans Conried. Gr 1-3. Houghton Mifflin.

R   Just So Stories Disc Series, Volume 1. Gr 4-6. Nine stories. Spoken Arts.

R   "Louisa May Alcott's *Little Women,* Chapters 1 and 2." Gr 3-7. CMS.

T   Meet the Authors Series. Gr 4-8. Twenty items in the series, including interviews with Arna Bontemps, Marguerite Henry, and Lloyd Alexander. Imperial Productions.

R   Newbery Award Records Series. Gr 4-9. Twelve books in the series, including *Call It Courage* and *Johnny Tremain.* Newbery Award Records.

T   "Nursery Rhymes." Gr K-2. Two records. Teaching Technology.

R   Poetry Parade Series. Gr 1-8. Two records on the poetry of David McCord, Harry Behn, Karla Kuskin and Aileen Fisher. Weston Woods.

T   Spoken Arts Cassette Library for Young Listeners Series. Gr K-3. Fifty items in the series, ranging from John Ciardi's poetry to fairy tales from Grimm's. Spoken Arts.

R   "The Three Billy Goats Gruff/The Gingerbread Man." Read by Bob Thomas and Jean Richards. Gr K-3. Folkways/Scholastic Records.

T   The Wind in the Willows Series. Gr 7-12. Teaching Technology.

R   "Uncle Remus Stories and Hans Christian Andersen Fairy Tales." Read by Frances Trotter and Ronven Stock. Gr 2-6. Toronto Public Library.

Directory of Record and Tape Sources

Alan Sands Productions, 565 Fifth Ave., New York, N.Y. 10017.

Bloch and Company, 1010 Euclid Building, Cleveland, Ohio 44115.

Caedmon Records, 505 Eighth Ave., New York, N. Y. 10018.

CMS Records, 14 Warren St., New York, N. Y. 10007.

Columbia Records, Modern Learning Aids, 1212 Avenue of the Americas, New York, N. Y. 10036.

Folkways/Scholastic Records, 50 W. 44th St., New York, N. Y. 10036.

Houghton Mifflin Co., 110 Tremont St., Boston, Mass. 02107.

Imperial Productions, Inc., 247 W. Court St., Kankakee, Ill. 60901.

Newbery Award Records, Inc., 342 Madison Ave. New York, N. Y. 10017.

Spoken Arts, Inc., 59 Locust Ave., New Rochelle, N. Y. 10801.

Teaching Technology Corporation, 5520 Cleon Ave., North Hollywood, Calif. 91601.

Toronto Public Library, College and St. George Sts., Toronto 2-B, Ontario, Canada.

Weston Woods, Weston, Conn. 06880.

CHAPTER
3

How to Handle Choral Speaking

One of the more effective ways of interpreting literature orally is to use choral speaking, an activity in which many voices speak as one melodious, well-articulated unit. The materials are most often poetry, though rhythmic prose such as the Psalms is highly appropriate. At times the whole class may speak in unison; but usually there are subgroupings of children who speak responsively. Often a class is divided into halves, each group speaking in alternation with the other; but there may be solos, duets, quartets, or any other type of grouping that will achieve a desired result. The leader, with the help of the children, works out groupings and arrangements which will best interpret the mood and meaning of the various selections to be spoken.

There are four basic types of choral speaking: the *refrain*, the *line-a-child*, the *antiphonal*, and *unison*. The next section of the chapter presents specific directions for teaching each of these types. At the end of the chapter is a section consisting of a large number of poems which can be used by choral speaking groups.

Major Types of Choral Arrangements

The four types of choral speaking are presented in order of difficulty, the easier ones first. For each type, three poems are used in demonstration so as to make the directions more explicit. The first poem is suitable for use in primary grades, the second in middle grades, and the last for seventh grade up.

Refrain

In this simplest type of choral arrangement, the teacher or leader speaks most of the lines while the class as a whole speaks together the repetitious words that constitute a refrain.

In introducing a poem to be used in choral speaking, the teacher endeavors to make the verse as appealing as he can. He sets the stage by recalling a recent lesson or school activity that is closely related, reminds the children of a current holiday, holds up a colorful picture that parallels the content of the poem, or otherwise stirs the interest and curiosity of his pupils. He then reads the poem as expressively as he can, with particular care to say the words of the refrain exactly as he plans to have the children say them. After a brief discussion to sharpen imagery and highlight meanings, the pupils are asked to listen a second time with particular attention to the words that constitute the refrain. They are asked to note the timing and intonations to use when they speak the refrain. Then, during the teacher's third reading, the children chime in softly.

If all the voices are to blend in one pleasing whole, the pupils must keep together, not only in rate of speaking but in their inflections and volume. To accomplish harmonious effects, the leader should use both his hands to direct the speaking just as he might in teaching a rote song. One hand should beat the rhythm and indicate just when to start and how fast to go. The other should be lifted as the volume is to increase, and lowered to indicate a decrease.

The teacher should never hurry his reading, even for those lines requiring a relatively quick tempo. In the first two poems that follow, note that the opening of each calls for slow, relatively vigorous speech; the closing should be spoken in a lighter voice and at a quicker rate. The words in "Bugle Song," too, give leads to what pitch and quality of voice are appropriate—slower and more emphatic in the beginning, clear and sweet and more subdued in the latter part.

The capital letters that precede certain lines indicate who is to speak the respective lines. The *T* stands for teacher or leader; the *P* for the pupil or persons repeating the refrain.

CLOCKS

T: Slowly ticks the big clock:
P: Tick-tock, tick-tock!
T: But Cuckoo Clock ticks a double quick:
P: Tick-a-tocka, tick-a-tocka,
      Tick-a-tocka, tick!

Unknown

THE MILKMAN'S HORSE

T: On summer mornings when it's hot,
      The milkman's horse can't even trot,
      But pokes along like this—
P: Klip-klop, klip-klop, klip-klop.

T: But in the winter brisk,
      He perks right up and wants to frisk,
      And then he goes like this—
P: Klipity-klop, klipity-klop, klipity-klop.
      Klipity, klipity, klop.

Unknown

BUGLE SONG

T: The splendor falls on castle walls
         And snowy summits old in story;
      The long light shakes across the lakes,
         And the wild cataract leaps in glory;
P: Blow, bugle, blow; set the wild echoes flying,
         Blow, bugle; answer, echoes, dying, dying, dying.

T: O hark, O hear! how thin and clear,
         And thinner, clearer, farther going!
      O sweet and far from cliff and scar
         The horns of Elfland blowing!
P: Blow, let us hear the purple glens replying:
         Blow, bugle; answer, echoes, dying, dying, dying.

T: O love, they die in yon rich sky,
         They faint on hill or field or river:
      Our echoes roll from soul to soul,
         And grow forever and forever.
P: Blow, bugle, blow; set the wild echoes flying,
         And answer, echoes, answer, dying, dying, dying.

Alfred, Lord Tennyson

Later in the chapter appear several pages of poems that feature refrains suitable for use in choral speaking. These, in general, are arranged so that the ones suitable for the youngest children come first and the more mature ones toward the end.

Line-a-Child Arrangements

Another easily directed type of choral speaking is the line-a-child or line-a-group. Here a single child (or a group of two to four children) speaks a line or a couplet; then another individual or group picks up and continues, one after another. It is necessary that the poem have lines or couplets that end with semicolons or periods (sometimes commas) so that thoughts are not broken up by assigning different parts to individuals or small groups. Vachel Lindsay's "The Little Turtle" is a good example. Note the structure of the following poems and the proposed arrangements.

BOW, WOW, SAYS THE DOG

P1:   Bow, wow, says the dog;
P2:   Mew, mew, says the cat;
P3:   Grunt, grunt, says the pig;
P4:   And squeak, says the rat;
P5:   Tu, whu, says the owl;
P6:   Caw, caw, goes the crow;
P7:   Quack, quack, goes the duck;
P8:   And moo, moo, says the cow.

Mother Goose

ONLY ONE MOTHER

P1:   Hundreds of stars in the deep blue sky,
P2:   Hundreds of shells on the shore together,
P3:   Hundreds of birds that go singing by,
P4:   Hundreds of lambs in the sunny weather.
P5:   Hundreds of dewdrops to greet the dawn,
P6:   Hundreds of bees in the purple clover,
P7:   Hundreds of butterflies on the lawn,
All: But only one mother the wide world over.

George Cooper

PIPPA'S SONG

P^1:   The year's at the spring
P^2:   And day's at the morn;
P^3:   Morning's at seven;
P^4:   The hillside's dew-pearled;
P^5:   The lark's on the wing;
P^6:   The snail's on the thorn;
P^7:   God's in his heaven—
All: All's right with the world.

Robert Browning

Each of the *P*'s preceding the lines represents an individual or small group who is to speak that line. Note that the last line in the second and third poems are to be spoken in unison. Though the lines in "Only One Mother" end with commas, and not with semicolons or periods, each line is nonetheless a separate idea that can of itself be spoken by a different individual or group.

In spite of the fact that each line or couplet in poems suitable for line-a-child treatment has something of a separate entity, there is an overall unity. This means that the leader must be very careful in his introductory reading to maintain the continuity of the poem as a whole. He does this by keeping his voice suspended at the end of every line until a period is reached. Otherwise, the voice of the child or group saying each line might drop in such a way as to break the poem up into bits and so lose the general meaning.

The teacher will introduce each poem in such an interesting and apt way that it will seem a natural part of the curriculum. After the first listening and the follow-up discussion to add to appreciation and understanding, the teacher will explain how to do a line-a-child arrangement and will assign parts to the various children. They will then listen a second time to see how the poem as a whole should sound, which words are to be emphasized and how, and what the rate of speaking is to be. It is wise in the beginning to have single pupils say the respective lines and to have them stand in the order of their production so that it will be easier to "keep things moving" and not lose the overall meaning. If later the teacher wishes to have small groups take turns in saying the lines, he should direct as he did in the refrain type: showing the tempo of speaking with one hand, and the volume of the voices with the other.

Antiphonal Speaking

This type of choral speaking is very old, historically speaking. In early times the people of Palestine and Greece chanted back and forth from the hillsides of their natural amphitheatres. The Psalms, in many instances, are intended for this responsive production; and many churches retain in their services the responsive readings in which the pastor and the congregation take turns in speaking the lines. As may already be evident, antiphonal speaking involves alternate speaking by two or more groups.

This is the most important and common type of choral speaking. In the beginning, it is simply alternation between two groups, possibly the boys and the girls. In the end, with older and more experienced speakers, it may culminate in a verse choir with voices grouped according to pitch—low, average, high if in three parts; very low, low, average, high, very high if in as many as five parts. These multi-pitch groups may alternate or combine in various ways so as to get harmonious and varied effects that contribute to an effective interpretation of the poem. Group speaking can be supplemented by solo and small-group parts to lend an "anthem" effect.

To teach antiphonally, the teacher must plan carefully ahead of time in order to decide the kind of groupings to make for a poem and to determine how to divide it among the groups. Here are some basic suggestions, most of which are demonstrated in the three poems.

1. Start with question-and-answer kinds of poems in which the heavier voices (possibly the boys') ask the questions.
2. Use poems written as dialogue. If any of the parts have predominantly long vowels, the heavier voices should take them.
3. Find poems featuring contrasts. The more vigorous sections should be carried by the heavier voices. (See "Laughter.")

4. In the beginning, use only two groups: boys and girls, or low-pitched voices and high-pitched ones.

THREE LITTLE MICE

Three little mice sat down to spin,
Pussy passed by and she peeped in.
"What are you doing, my little men?"
"We're making coats for gentlemen."
"Shall I come in and bite off your threads?"
"No, no, Miss Pussy, you'll bite off our heads."
"Oh, no, I'll not. I'll help you spin."
"That may be so, but you don't come in."

Mother Goose

WHISTLE, MAMIE

I: Whistle, Mamie, whistle;
      I'll give you a cow.
II: I can't whistle;
      I don't know how.

I: Whistle, Mamie, whistle;
      I'll give you a pig.
II: I can't whistle;
      I'm too big.

I: Whistle, Mamie, whistle;
      I'll give you a man.
II: I can't — Whee! —
      Yes, I guess I can!

Unknown

LAUGHTER

I: The North Wind laughs with a loud Ho! Ho!
II: The South Wind laughs with a Whee!
I: The snowman laughs at the swirling snow
II: And some folks laugh at *me!*

II: Fairies laugh with a tinkling laugh
      Which sounds like a fairy bell.
I: And goblins snicker and laugh He! He!
      At the secrets which goblins tell.

II: When the little Easter bunny laughs,
      He wrinkles up his nose;
I: And the clown in the circus laughs out loud
      As round the ring he goes.

Unknown

In the preceding poems, the Roman numeral *I* stands for the group with the heavier voices and the *II* indicates the parts for the lighter voices. As usual, the leader will introduce the poem, have it talked over only as much as necessary to clear up meanings, explain how to do the antiphonal speaking, assign parts, and read a second time as each group listens carefully for intonations, pauses, and rate of speaking. Careful direction by the leader is especially important in antiphonal speaking. In the beginning, the teacher should read and the pupils chime in softly not once, but several times. After each rendition, he should demonstrate again any phrases or lines that need improved expression. Because a poem to be spoken antiphonally needs to be worked on so much, it must be a poem of truly high calibre, which the children are unlikely to grow tired of.

In preparing to teach "Three Little Mice" to younger children, the leader should work on his own enunciation and indicate carefully which words need emphasis. Conversation like that in this poem is usually easy to teach because the children use naturally the intonations they would in real-life dialogue. The first two lines may be said in unison. If this is done, the leader should insist that the children enunciate clearly and that they keep their voices exactly together; only then will there be incisive effects.

"Whistle, Mamie" calls for lifelike intonations. It is an easy poem to teach. "Laughter," however, will get pleasing effects only if the voices are carefully separated into two pitches —deep and light. In his first reading of the poem the leader should vary the pitch and volume of his voice to indicate the respective parts for the two types of voices. In addition, he should carefully maintain continuity throughout the poem, and should be particularly careful at the end of each line having no punctuation. While proper phrasing of word groups in the poem justifies a pause at the end of such lines, the voice must be kept suspended to indicate continuity. To ensure a smooth and melodious blending of the pupils' voices, the leader should read the poem several times as they listen carefully for inflections, volume, and timing. Before each reading, he should ask them to listen for some special aspect of expression as, for example, smooth continuity at the end of each line, or words to be emphasized, in order to attain an effective interpretation.

As a rule, antiphonal speaking is used in the middle grades and above. (Primary children may do some group speaking because they so enjoy it; but they are not held to the precision that true antiphonal speaking calls for.) At first, the teacher sets a "pattern" by his oral reading, and the children imitate this as precisely as possible. However, after they have had experience in speaking several poems in antiphonal fashion, they may assume some responsibility for planning and demonstrating how a poem is to be spoken. Each of several children will read it orally; the class will choose the interpretation they prefer; they will listen to the chosen child read it two or three times so that they may repeat the poem in exactly the same manner. (There has to be an agreement on inflections, timing, and tone of voice before the groups begin to practice on antiphonal speaking. Only in that way can smooth and clear-cut effects be secured.)

For the teacher to plan appropriate arrangements, the children must be given an understanding of certain policies. Here are some of them: (1) The lighter voices will ask the questions in a question-answer type of poem; (2) In dialogue boys will take the parts spoken by men or boys; (3) If one side of a dialogue or alternate lines or couplets have predominantly long-vowel sounds, the heavier voices will take over such parts; (4) The "dark" emotions, such as despair or deep anger, should be portrayed by low-pitched voices. Lighthearted parts call for high-pitched voices; (5) Strength and vigor are best expressed by heavier voices.

A verse choir is the ultimate in effective choral speaking. A leader without considerable training in speech or music should be cautious about organizing and directing a verse choir because such activity calls for real expertise. Pupils, too, should have become quite expert in interpreting verse in choral fashion before they are used in a verse choir. Usually such choirs involve only high school or college students, though well-trained junior high school pupils with pronounced ability can do well. Selections for verse choirs are often quite lengthy and are most certainly involved. It takes skills acquired in specialized training to plan and effect arrangements for a verse choir. There will be from three to four groups, each representing a different voice quality from very light to very deep. We might say that the teacher tests to determine who are the sopranos, altos, tenors, and baritones among her pupils. Then a poem must be analyzed to see which parts of it should be assigned to each voice-group or given over to solos, duets, or quartets. After many rehearsals to get well-integrated effects, the verse choir may succeed in attaining melodious, meaningful interpretations that may well be dubbed "spoken anthems."

Unison

In the unison type of choral speaking, an entire group speaks lines together. There is no subgrouping. This type may seem to be simple, but actually it is the hardest of all to direct in such a way as to get precision and beauty. Only a truly skillful leader can direct a large number of voices speaking simultaneously in a way that will get parallel inflections, perfect timing, and consistent voice quality. Usually pupils speaking in unison repeat only a part of the lines in a poem. However, short poems like the following can be entirely unison.

HERE WE GO

Here we go up, up, up,
And here we go down, down, downy;
Here we go backwards and forwards,
And here we go round, round, roundy.

Old rhyme

GOOD NIGHT

Good night! Good night!
Far flies the light;
But still God's love
Shall flame above,
Making all bright.
Good night! Good night!

Victor Hugo

WEATHER

Whether the weather be fine,
Or whether the weather be not,
Whether the weather be cold
Or whether the weather be hot,
We'll weather the weather,
Whatever the weather,
Whether we like it or not.

Unknown

Technically, primary children should not participate in much unison speaking because it is so hard to coordinate their voices. However, young children can get so much pleasure out of saying nursery rhymes and other simple tuneful poems together that most teachers let them say bits of verse in unison. In "Here We Go" the pupils not only speak together but, after they know the poem well, act it out as they repeat it. In the first reading, the teacher should set a rhythm which can control the timing of such actions as rising on tiptoes, lowering to regular position, stepping forward and backward, and turning about. It would be well for the teacher to prepare for teaching by rehearsing the motions as he says the poem to himself. Then he can be assured of proper timing in his initial presentation to the children.

The famous poem, "Good Night," calls for a reverently deep tone and a somewhat slow rendition. Note that there should be no pause between lines 3 and 4. In speaking "Weather," the teacher should bring out the contrasts between fine weather and "not," between cold and hot. This poem is effective only as the contrasts in meaning are carefully brought out by higher inflections and emphatic speaking. There should be an air of humor and I-don't-careness in saying it.

Children enjoy acting out poems as they speak the words. Among the poems at the end of the chapter is "The Grand Old Duke of York." After the children are thoroughly familiar with the words, one half of the class can march to the words as their classmates repeat the poem. Naturally the rhythm of the words will be somewhat exaggerated. In anthologies teachers may find other poems about hippity-hopping, swinging, and other active motion—poems in which the authors have tried to have the rhythm of words and actions correspond. Having such verse pantomimed while a portion of a class speaks the words in unison is a very interesting activity. Nursery rhymes like "Little Miss Muffet" and "Little Jack Horner" may also be acted out, though the pantomiming need not be rhythmic as in the aforementioned poems.

General Suggestions for Selecting Poems

In selecting poems to use in choral speaking, possibly the most important criterion for choice is that the literature and materials chosen be so high in quality, tuneful and/or clever that the children will not tire of them during the many repetitions necessary in practicing to achieve precision. Nursery rhymes, which have lasted through the centuries, are good for the youngest children. Poems that feature strong contrast are especially suitable for division into parts to be spoken by voices that differ in pitch. "Laughter" is a good example. Children also like poetry that is narrative, full of action, or humorous. Of course the more musical the words and phrasing, the better. Rhyming patterns, alliteration, and a pleasing rhythm add to the appeal of poetry. As has been said, some prose that has a sweeping rhythm, melodious words, and vivid word pictures is suitable material for choral speaking. The best example is the Psalms.

Poems for Practice

This section of chapter 3 presents a number of poems suitable for choral speaking. It is divided into four parts, one for each type of presentation. Within each part, the poems are generally arranged from the easiest ones for the youngest to the harder ones for adolescents. No arrangements are suggested. In planning how to teach children to speak any one poem in choral style, the leader should note in which category it is listed and then turn back to the preceding pages where the directions for teaching that type of choral arrangement are given. (Page numbers for reference are given with the category titles as they appear in the text following.) Another check of the three demonstration poems in the corresponding type of choral speaking should also be helpful.

Refrain (refer to pages 49-51)

These poems feature refrains which are to be spoken by the entire group while the teacher or another expert leader speaks the remainder of the poem. Direct the group so that the enunciation is as clear as if a single voice were saying the refrain.

MIAU! MIAU!

"Who's that ringing at the front door bell?"
Miau! Miau! Miau!
"I'm a little Pussy Cat and I'm not very well!"
Miau! Miau! Miau!

"Then rub your nose in a bit of mutton fat."
Miau! Miau! Miau!
"For that's the way to cure a little Pussy Cat."
Miau! Miau! Miau!

Old rhyme

BELLS

The big bell sings,
  "Ding, dong; ding, dong!
I'm very proud
  Of my deep, deep song."

The little bell sings,
  "Ting-a-ling-ling-ling,
When you keep still,
  Then I can sing."

Unknown

DOODLE DOODLE DOO

Doodle doodle doo,
The princess lost her shoe;
  Her highness hopped—
  The fiddler stopped,
Not knowing what to do.
Doodle doodle doo.

Mother Goose

MY HORSE

My horse can gallop,
  My horse can trot,
Clippety, clappety,
  Gallop-a-trot.
And he'd like a rider
  As well as not,
Clippety, clappety,
  Gallop-a-trot.

Mother Goose

AUTUMN LEAVES

The autumn leaves are dancing down,
  Dance, leaves, dance!
Leaves of crimson, gold and brown,
  Dance, leaves, dance!
Let the wind whirl you around,
Make a carpet for the ground;
Soon you'll sleep without a sound.
  Dance, leaves, dance!

Unknown

LITTLE BROWN RABBIT

Little brown rabbit went hoppity-hop,
Hoppity-hop, hoppity-hop!
Into a garden without any stop,
Hoppity-hop, hoppity-hop!

He ate for his supper a fresh carrot top,
Hoppity-hop, hoppity-hop!
Then home went the rabbit without any stop,
Hoppity-hop, hoppity-hop!

Unknown

THE MERRY ROBIN

Out in an apple tree there he was swinging,
Out in an apple tree, whistling, singing,
"Morning! Morning! Good morning!"

Never a harsh note, never a sad one,
Always a jolly note, always a glad one,
"Morning! Morning! Good morning!"

Wait, Mr. Robin, I will sing with you;
Let me go merrily right along with you,
"Morning! Morning! Good morning!"

Leland Jacobs

Permisson granted by F. A. Owen Publishing Co.

WE THANK THEE

For flowers so beautiful and sweet,
For friends and clothes and food to eat,
For precious hours, for work and play,
We thank Thee this Thanksgiving Day.

For father's care and mother's love,
For the blue sky and clouds above,
For springtime and for autumn gay,
We thank Thee this Thanksgiving Day.

For all Thy gifts so good and fair,
Bestowed so freely everywhere,
Give us grateful hearts we pray,
To thank Thee this Thanksgiving Day.

Unknown

INDIAN DANCE

Come on, Indians, dance and play;
Let us hear your tom-toms say,
BOM, BOM, BOM, BOM!
bom, bom, bom, bom!

Bend your head and stamp the ground;
Keep on dancing round and round—
BOM, bom, bom, bom!
BOM, bom, bom, bom!

Dorothy Dawson Lowell

STORM

What does the hail say?
  Knock! Knock!
What does the rain say?
  Pit, pat.
What does the sleet say?
  Sh, sh-h.
What does the wind say?
  Whoo! Whoo-oo!

Unknown

TRY, TRY AGAIN

'Tis a lesson you should heed,
  Try, try again;
If at first you don't succeed,
  Try, try again.
Then your courage should appear,
For, if you will persevere,
You will conquer, never fear;
  Try, try again.

T. H. Palmer

FLAG SONG

Out on the breeze
O'er land and seas,
A beautiful banner is streaming;
  Shining its stars,
  Splendid its bars,
Under the sunshine 'tis gleaming.
  Hail to the flag,
  The dear, bonny flag —
The flag that is red, white, and blue.
  Over the brave
  Long may it wave,
Peace to the world ever bringing,
  While to the stars
  Linked with the bars
Hearts will forever be singing:
  Hail to the flag,
  The dear, bonny flag—
The flag that is red, white, and blue.

Lydia Avery Ward

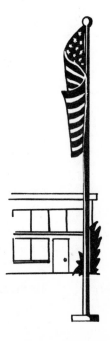

POOR OLD WOMAN

There was on old woman who swallowed a fly.
Oh, my! Swallowed a fly!
Poor old woman, I think she'll die.

There was an old woman who swallowed a spider;
Right down inside her she swallowed a spider;
She swallowed the spider to kill the fly.
Oh, my! Swallowed a fly!
Poor old woman, I think she'll die.

There was an old woman who swallowed a bird.
How absurd to swallow a bird!
She swallowed the bird to kill the spider,
She swallowed the spider to kill the fly.
Oh, my! Swallowed a fly!
Poor old woman, I think she'll die.

There was an old woman who swallowed a cat,
Fancy that! She swallowed a cat!
She swallowed the cat to kill the bird
She swallowed the bird to kill the spider,
She swallowed the spider to kill the fly.
Oh, my! Swallowed a fly!
Poor old woman, I think she'll die.

There was an old woman who swallowed a dog.
She went the whole hog! She swallowed a dog!
She swallowed the dog to kill the cat,
She swallowed the cat to kill the bird,
She swallowed the bird to kill the spider,
She swallowed the spider to kill the fly.
Oh, my! Swallowed a fly!
Poor old woman, I think she'll die.

There was an old woman who swallowed a cow,
I don't know how, but she swallowed a cow.
She swallowed the cow to kill the dog,
She swallowed the dog to kill the cat,
She swallowed the cat to kill the bird,
She swallowed the bird to kill the spider,
She swallowed the spider to kill the fly.
Oh, my! Swallowed a fly!
Poor old woman, I think she'll die.

There was an old woman who swallowed a horse!
She died, of course.

Unknown

Line-a-Child (refer to pages 51-53)

A different child will say each line or couplet for most of the poems reproduced here. The teacher or some other expert leader may be responsible for the lines that start or end the poems where line-a-child effects are not appropriate.

FIVE KITTENS

Five furry kittens waiting in the house—
Softly! Softly!
They think they hear a mouse.
The white kitten says, "Be still!"
The gray kitten says, "We will!"
The brown kitten says, "Oh, where?"
The striped kitten says, "Right there!"
The black kitten says, "Take care!"
"Squeak!" went the mouse—
And they all ran under the house.

Unknown

FARMER'S DAY

When the farmer's day is done,
In the barnyard, ev'ry one,
Beast and bird politely say,
"Thank you for my food today."
The cow says, "Moo!"
The pigeon, "Coo!"
The sheep says, "Baa!"
The lamb says, "Maa!"
The hen, "Cluck! Cluck!"
"Quack!" says the duck;
The dog, "Bow-wow!"
The cat, "Meow!"
The horse says, "Neigh!
I love my sweet hay!
The pig near by
Grunts in his sty.
When the barn is locked up right,
Then the farmer says, "Good night!"
Thanks his animals, ev'ry one,
For the work that has been done.

Maude Burnham

FIVE CHICKENS

Said the first little chicken,
  With a queer little squirm,
"I wish I could find
  A fat little worm."

Said the next little chicken,
  With an odd little shrug,
"I wish I could find
  A fat little slug."

Said the third little chicken,
  With a sharp little squeal,
"I wish I could find
  Some nice yellow meal."

Said the fourth little chicken,
  With a small sigh of grief,
"I wish I could find
  A little green leaf."

Said the fifth little chicken,
  With a faint little moan,
"I wish I could find
  A wee gravel stone."

"Now, see here," said the mother,
  From the green garden patch,
"If you want any breakfast,
  Just come here and scratch."

Unknown

FUNNY

Wouldn't it be funny—
  Wouldn't it now?
If the dog said, "Moo-oo"
  And the cow said, "Bow-wow?"
If the cat sang and whistled
  And the bird said, "Mia-ow?"
Wouldn't it be funny—
  Wouldn't it now?

Unknown

FIVE LITTLE SQUIRRELS

Five little squirrels
  Sat in a tree
The first one said,
  "What do I see?"
The second one said,
  "A man with a gun."
The third one said,
  "We'd better run."
The fourth one said,
  "Let's hide in the shade."
The fifth one said,
  "I'm not afraid."
Then BANG went the gun,
And how they did run!

Unknown

How Creatures Move

The lion walks on padded paws,
    The squirrel leaps from limb to limb,
While flies can crawl straight up a wall
    And seals can dive and swim.
The long worm wiggles all around,
    The monkey swings by his tail
And birds may hop upon the ground
    Or spread their wings and sail.
        But boys and girls
            Have much more fun;
        They leap and dance
            And walk and run.

Unknown

Everywhere, Christmas

Everywhere, everywhere, Christmas tonight!
Christmas in lands of the fir tree and pine,
Christmas in lands of the palm tree and vine,
Christmas where snow peaks stand solemn and white,
Christmas where cornfields stand sunny and bright.
Christmas where children are hopeful and gay,
Christmas where old men are patient and gray,
Christmas where peace, like a dove in his flight,
Broods over brave men in the thick of the fight;
Everywhere, everywhere, Christmas tonight!
For the Christ-Child who comes is the Master of all;
No place too great, no cottage too small.

Phillips Brooks

If All the Seas

If all the seas were one sea,
What a great sea that would be!
And if all the trees were one tree,
What a great tree that would be!
And if all the axes were one axe,
What a great axe that would be!
And if all the men were one man,
What a great man that would be!
And if the great man took the great axe,
And cut down the great tree,
And let it fall into the great sea,
What a splish splash that would be!

Mother Goose

Loss

For want of a nail, the shoe was lost;
For want of the shoe, the horse was lost;
For want of a horse, the rider was lost;
For want of the rider, the battle was lost;
For want of the battle, the kingdom was lost;
All for the want of a horseshoe nail.

Traditional

Glad Things

Of glad things there be four, aye four:
A lark above the old nest blithely singing,
A wild rose clinging
In safety to a rock, a shepherd bringing
A lamb found in his arms,
And Christmas bells a-ringing.

Unknown

Antiphonal (refer to pages 53-57)

Here two groups of children take turns speaking their
parts. The lighter voices ask the questions, say the gayer lines,
or repeat the lines with the most short-vowel sounds.

Fish Bite

1, 2, 3, 4, 5,
I caught a fish alive;
6, 7, 8, 9, 10,
I let it go again.
Why did you let it go?
Because it bit my finger so.
Which finger did it bite?
The little finger on the right.
    Oh!   Oh!   Oh!

Mother Goose

Autumn

Autumn is here,
King of the year,
Painting the landscape with gold;
Flowers and trees
Dance with the bees,
Whispering secrets ne'er told.
Cobwebs are flying,
Birds all day crying,
Jack Frost comes crisp and cold.

Henry A. Bamman

Bell Horses

Bell horses, bell horses,
What time of day?
One o'clock, two o'clock,
Three—and away!

Mother Goose

Two Blackbirds

There were two blackbirds
  Sitting on a hill,
The one named Jack,
  The other named Jill.

Fly away, Jack;
  Fly away, Jill;
Come again, Jack;
  Come again, Jill.

Mother Goose

Pussy Cat

Pussy-cat, pussy-cat,
  Where have you been?
I've been to London
  To visit the queen.

Pussy-cat, pussy-cat,
  What did you there?
I frightened a little mouse
  Under the chair.

Mother Goose

To London Town

"Which is the way to London Town,
To see the King in his golden crown?"
"One foot up and one foot down,
That's the way to London Town."

"What is the way to London Town,
To see the Queen in her silken gown?"
"Left! Right! Left! Right! up and down,
Soon you'll be in London Town!"

Old rhyme

Soap Bubbles

Fill the pipe!
  Gently blow;
Now you'll see
  The bubbles grow!
Strong at first,
Then they burst,
Then they go
To nothing, oh!

Unknown

Doing

What does the bee do?
  Bring home honey.
What does Father do?
  Bring home money.
And what does Mother do?
  Pay out the money.
And what does Baby do?
  Eat up the honey.

Mother Goose

White Sheep

White sheep, white sheep,
  On a blue hill,
When the wind stops
  You all stand still.
When the wind blows
  You walk away slow.
White sheep, white sheep,
  Where do you go?

Unknown

Two Little Menikin

Peter and Michael were two little menikin,
They kept a cook and a fat little henikin;
Instead of an egg, it laid a gold penikin,
Oh, how they wish it would do it againikin.

Old rhyme

Little Robin Redbreast

Little Robin Redbreast
  Sat upon a rail;
Niddle-naddle went his head,
  Wiggle-waggle went his tail.

Little Robin Redbreast
  Sat upon a tree,
Up went Pussy Cat,
  And down went he;

Down came Pussy Cat,
  And away Robin ran;
Said little Robin Redbreast,
  "Catch me if you can."

Little Robin Redbreast
  Jumped upon a wall;
Pussy Cat jumped after him,
  And almost had a fall.

Little Robin Redbreast chirped and sang,
  And what did the pussy say?
Pussy Cat said, "Mew,"
  And Robin jumped away.

Mother Goose

TWO CATS OF KILKENNY

There were once two cats of Kilkenny,
Each thought there was one cat too many;
So they fought and they fit,
And they scratched and they bit,
Till, excepting their nails
And the tips of their tails,
Instead of two cats, there weren't any.

Anonymous

MERRY MAY

Merry, rollicking, frolicking May
Into the wood came skipping one day;
She teased the brook till he laughed outright,
And gurgled and scolded with all his might;
She chirped to the birds and bade them sing
A chorus of welcome to Lady Spring;
And the bees and the butterflies she set
To waking the flowers that were sleeping yet.
She shook the trees till the buds looked out
To see what the trouble was all about,
And nothing in Nature escaped that day
The touch of life-giving bright young May.

George Macdonald

COURAGE

Three things have taught me courage—
Three things I've seen today:
A spider reweaving her web
Which thrice had been swept away;
A child refusing to weep
In spite of cruel pain;
A robin singing a cheering song
In the midst of a chilling rain.

Charles Albertson

A DAY IN JUNE

And what is so rare as a day in June?
Then, if ever, come perfect days;
Then Heaven tries earth if it be in tune,
And over it softly her warm ear lays:
Whether we look, or whether we listen,
We hear life murmur, or see it glisten;
Every clod feels a stir of might,
An instinct within it that reaches and towers,
And, groping blindly above it for light,
Climbs to a soul in grass and flowers.

James Russell Lowell

NIGHT SKIES

All day long
The sun shines bright.
The moon and stars
Come out at night.
From twilight time
They line the skies
And watch the world with quiet eyes.

Unknown

Unison (refer to pages 57-58)

In this most difficult of the types of choral speaking, an entire group speaks verse together. It is recommended that a class should be divided into groups of twelve, each group to prepare a different poem. It is no simple task to keep more than twelve children together in precisely identical enunciation, word groupings, and intonation.

GRAND OLD DUKE OF YORK

O, the grand old Duke of York,
He had ten thousand men;
He marched them up a very high hill,
And he marched them down again.
And when they were up, they were up,
And when they were down, they were down;
And when they were only half way up,
They were neither up nor down.

Nursery Rhyme

STOP! LOOK! LISTEN!

Stop! Look and listen
  Before you cross the street.
Use your eyes; use your ears;
  Then use your feet.

Unknown

MAY DAY

On May Day we dance
On May Day we sing;
For this is the day
  We welcome the spring.

Old rhyme

LINDA'S LOCKET

Little Linda lost her locket,
Lovely, lucky, little locket.
Lately Linda found her locket
Lying still in Linda's pocket.

Unknown

CROOKED

There was a crooked man, and he went a crooked mile
And found a crooked sixpence against a crooked stile;
He bought a crooked cat that caught a crooked mouse,
And they all lived together in a little crooked house.

Mother Goose

RAIN

Rain is a rascal
  Who slips down the lanes.
He races with sunshine
  And taps window panes.
He dances in puddles
  And trips down the street;
And when it turns cold,
  He turns into sleet.

Elaine von Ruedon

All You Can

Do all the good you can,
By all the means you can,
In all the ways you can,
In all the places you can,
At all the times you can,
To all the people you can,
As long as ever you can.

Traditional

Be Like the Bird

Be like the bird, who
Halting in his flight
On limb too slight
Feels it give way beneath him,
Yet sings
Knowing he hath wings.

Victor Hugo

The Bells

Hear the sledges with the bells—silver bells!
What a world of merriment their melody foretells.
How they tinkle, tinkle, tinkle in the icy air of night!
While the stars that oversprinkle
All the heavens seem to twinkle with a crystalline delight;
Keeping time, time, time, with a sort of Runic rhyme
To the tintinabulation that so musically wells
From the bells, bells, bells, bells,
  Bells, bells, bells, —
From the jingling and tinkling of the bells.

Edgar Allen Poe

A Thing of Beauty

A thing of beauty is a joy forever;
Its loveliness increases; it will never
Pass into nothingness; but still will keep
A bower quiet for us, and a sleep
Full of sweet dreams and health,
  And quiet breathing.

John Keats

SHOES

The frost wears silver slippers;
The rain wears mouse grey shoes,
But the ragged wind goes barefoot
And wades in shining dews.

Unknown

MILKWEED SEEDS

In a milkweed cradle,
    Snug and warm,
Baby seeds are hiding,
    Safe from harm.
Open wide the cradle,
    Hold it high!
Come, Mr. Wind!
    Help them fly.

Unknown

OPPORTUNITY

A curve in the wood, a hillside
    Clear cut against the sky,
A tall tree tossed by the autumn wind,
    A white cloud riding high:

Ten men went along that road
    And all but one passed by—
He saw the hill, the tree and the cloud
    With an artist's mind and eye.
So he set them down on canvas
    For the other nine men to buy.

Anonymous

The heavens are telling the glory of God; and the firmament proclaims his handiwork. Day to day pours forth speech, and night to night declares knowledge. There is no speech, nor are there words; their voice is not heard; yet their voice goes forth through all the earth; and their words to the end of the world.

Psalm 19

Selections for Choral Speaking

Primary: Refrain

The Baby Goes to Boston (*Laura E. Richards*)
Bow Wow Wow
Cock-a-Doodle Do
The Christmas Pudding (*Unknown*)
Hickory Dickory Dock
Hippity Hop to Bed (*Leroy Jackson*)
Hoppity (*A. A. Milne*)
The Mitten Song (*Mary Louise Allen*)
Sleep, Baby, Sleep
There Were Two Birds Sat Upon a Stone
This Is the Way the Ladies Ride
To Market, to Market

Primary: Line-a-Child

Jump or Jiggle (*Evelyn Beyer*)
The Little Turtle (*Vachel Lindsay*)
Little Wind (*Kate Greenaway*)
One, Two, Buckle My Shoe
This Little Pig Went to Market

Primary: Antiphonal

Baa, Baa, Black Sheep
Ding Dong Bell
Good Morning (*Muriel Sipe*)
Little Boy Blue
The Little Kittens (*Eliza Lee Follen*)
Merry-Go-Round (*Dorothy Baruch*)
Mousie, Mousie
My Zipper Suit (*Marie Louise Allen*)
The Squirrel (*Unknown*)
There Were Once Two Cats of Kilkenny
What Are Little Boys Made Of?
What Does Little Birdie Say? (*Alfred Tennyson*)

Primary: Unison

Birdie with a Yellow Bill
Blow, Wind, Blow

Daffadowndilly
Hey, Diddle Diddle
Humpty Dumpty
I Love Little Pussy (*Jane Taylor*)
Jack Be Nimble
Little Boy Blue
Little Jack Horner
Little Miss Muffet
Mix a Pancake
Pease Porridge
The Purple Cow (*Gelett Burgess*)
Rain, Rain, Go Away
The Swing (*Robert Louis Stevenson*)
There Was a Crooked Man
This Happy Day (*Harry Behn*)
White Sheep, White Sheep

Intermediate: Refrain

A Farmer Went Trotting
Husky Hi (*Rose Fyleman*)
The Light-Hearted Fairy
Little Gray Billy Goat
Long, Long Ago (*Unknown*)
The Wind (*Robert Louis Stevenson*)

Intermediate: Line-a-Child

Boys' Names (*Eleanor Farjeon*)
Fat Old Fluffy
Girls' Names (*Eleanor Farjeon*)
The Goblin (*Rose Fyleman*)
Mice (*Rose Fyleman*)
Some One (*Walter de la Mare*)
Susan Blue (*Kate Greenaway*)
What Do We Plant? (*Henry Abbey*)
Who Likes the Rain?

Intermediate: Antiphonal

Black and Gold (*Nancy Byrd Turner*)
Five Little Monkeys

Grasshopper Green
It Is Raining (*Lucy Sprague Mitchell*)
The Little Elf (*John Kendrick Bangs*)
The Sky Fairies
What Is Pink? (*Christina Rossetti*)
Who Has Seen the Wind? (*Christina Rossetti*)
The Wilderness Is Tamed (*Elizabeth Coatsworth*)
Winter Night (*Mary Frances Butts*)
The Wonderful World (*William B. Rands*)
Why Do Bells for Christmas Ring? (*Eugene Field*)

Intermediate: Unison

Autumn Woods (*James Tippett*)
Galoshes (*Rhoda Bacmeister*)
Grizzly Bear (*Mary Austin*)
Indian Lullaby (*Charles Myall*)
A Little Dutch Garden
Poor Tired Tim (*Walter de la Mare*)
There's a New Year Coming (*Lucy Larcom*)
Windy Nights (*Robert Louis Stevenson*)

Upper: Refrain

The Call of the Wind
I Heard a Bird Sing (*Oliver Herford*)
Merry Are the Bells (*Anonymous*)
Pop Corn Song

Upper: Line-a-Child

Godfrey Gordon Gustavus Gore (*William B. Rands*)
Hie Away (*Sir Walter Scott*)
Lone Dog (*Irene R. McLeod*)
Swift Things Are Beautiful (*Elizabeth Coatsworth*)
Trees (*Joyce Kilmer*)
Written in March (*William Wordsworth*)

Upper: Antiphonal

Afternoon on a Hill (*Edna St. V. Millay*)
America the Beautiful (*Katharine Lee Bates*)
Do You Fear the Wind? (*Hamlin Garland*)

The Flag Goes By (*Henry H. Bennett*)
Gregory Griggs
How Did You Take It? (*Edmund V. Cooke*)
Night (*Sara Teasdale*)
Opportunity (*Edward R. Sill*)

Upper: Unison

The Coin (*Sara Teasdale*)
Hats Off (*Henry H. Bennett*)
Hold Fast Your Dreams (*Louise Driscoll*)
Silver (*Walter de la Mare*)
Velvet Shoes (*Elinor Wylie*)

BIBLIOGRAPHY

ABNEY, LOUISE. *Choral Speaking Arrangements for the Lower Grades* (selected). Magnolia, Mass.: Expression Co., 1953.

————. *Choral Speaking Arrangements for the Upper Grades* (selected). Magnolia, Mass.: Expression Co., 1952.

ARBUTHNOT, MAY HILL. *Children and Books,* pp. 220-45. Chicago: Scott, Foresman, 1964.

BROWN, HELEN A., *et al. Choral Readings for Fun and Recreation.* Philadelphia: Westminster, 1956.

GULLEN, MARJORIE. *Choral Speaking.* London: Methuen, 1957.

JONES, MORRIS V. "Choral Speaking in the Elementary School." *Elementary English,* December 1958, pp. 535-37.

NELSON, RICHARD C. "Children's Poetry Preferences." *Elementary English,* March 1966, pp. 247-51.

NEUMANN, M. A. "Choral Reading with Pantomime." *Instructor,* December 1957, p. 39.

PITTMAN, GRACE. "Young Children Enjoy Poetry," *Elementary English,* January 1966, pp. 56-59.

PLACE, C. S. "Choral Reading with Music." *Grade Teacher,* September 1960, pp. 71; 121-22.

RASMUSSEN, CARRIE. "Choral Reading in the Elementary School." *NEA Journal.* November 1960, p. 26.

————. *Speech Methods in the Elementary School,* pp. 90-92, 234-39. New York: Ronald, 1949.

ROBINSON, EVELYN R. *Readings about Children's Literature,* pp. 407-9. New York: McKay, 1966.

WERNER, LORNA. *Speech in the Elementary School,* pp. 75-122; 205-7. Evanston, Ill.: Row, 1947.

CHAPTER 4

Creative Dramatics in the Elementary School

Dramatic activities are a part of a child's growing up, an important means for his learning to understand the adults around him and for his developing traits that will characterize his own later adulthood. As he plays house or school, acts out the stories he hears or reads, or dramatizes the events of history, he gains insight and develops traits that help in building his personality and basic character. While creative dramatics does have these serious and important values, it is also a means of recreation, of having fun. Play-acting is the essence of a child's being, a part of his normal way of life.

It is this original and uninhibited play-acting which serves as the wellspring of all the forms of dramatic expression in the elementary school. Here in basic form are all the dramatic elements of action, plot, and characterization which mark the finest plays. Any teacher who is alert will give recognition to this natural bent of children, and do his utmost to encourage and supplement it.

Creative dramatics in the elementary school can and should take varied forms, the nature of which tends to vary according to the child's stage of maturation. While there is no universal agreement on the exact form and advisable time allotment for dramatics at the successive grade levels, the following points reflect general practice: (1) informal dramatics, beginning with creative rhythms and unstructured dramatic play in the primary grades and gradually developing into informal portrayal of literary stories, both at the primary and intermediate levels; (2) pantomime and puppetry from the simplest stick puppets to the involved T-string type; and (3) formal play production employing involved plot, expressive dialogue, and personality-reflecting characterization at the upper reaches of the elementary school. It is generally agreed that each of these forms of expression has its place in the dramatics program of the elementary school. This chapter deals with these various forms of creative expression.

Rhythmic Activities

Rhythm is an intrinsic element in the dramatic arts, especially in the earliest school years. Throughout the elementary school period, rhythmic movement may be explored along two avenues—rhythm in coordinating bodily movements, and rhythmic response to music.

Rhythmic Movements

The kindergarten teacher starts the children off by encouraging them to express their ideas and feelings through bodily movements in such fundamental action as galloping, hopping, jumping, leaping, skipping, running, and walking in well-coordinated fashion. In all these rhythmic activities, the children are led to employ only gross bodily movements.

There is no one best way to begin. It is possible for the teacher to demonstrate a rhythm activity which the children will genuinely enjoy. He can thus set the tone for the future and help the children initiate new types of pleasurable rhythmic expression. Or, he may begin by allowing them the run of their imaginations so that their interpretations will be truly creative and expressive of their inherent feelings and thoughts. In any event, the teacher must remember to keep his plans for rhythmic activities simple and to center them on strong interests of children.

Dramatic play in itself evokes natural bodily movements and encourages rhythmic responses. The following list indicates some of the diverse, child-centered activities that give opportunities for smoothly coordinated movements.

Acting like mother, father, a policeman, *et al.*
Building a house, a bridge, a sand castle, *et al.*
Going to a picnic, the park, the beach, a farm, *et al.*
Impersonating a train, an airplane, a steam shovel, a toy, *et al.*
Playing house, store, hospital, *et al.*

A trip to the beach may form the basis for beginning activities in dramatic play. Prior to setting up the actual classroom situation, the teacher envisions the kinds of rhythmic movements the children can perform in order to express their ideas and feelings about the experiences at the beach. The dramatic activities might imitate the activities of wading in shallow water, swimming, riding in a motor boat or paddling a canoe, building a palace of sand or digging for clams, and other behavior at the beach. In his planning, the teacher considers whether he has included rhythmic activities involving most of the fundamental movements of the human body.

In the next step, actual teaching, the following dialogue might ensue:

Mrs. Laffter: How many of you went to the beach this summer? Well, so did I! I saw some people digging in the sand for crabs. How fast they had to work! This is the way they were digging. (*She acts as if she sees a crab about to disappear in the deep sand and begins to dig frantically.*)

Kay: I tried to dig some crabs too. They were too quick for me.

Mrs. Laffter: Show us how you dug, Kay. How did you act when the crabs got away? (*Kay depicts her behavior so well that many of her classmates want to join in. Their doing so is entirely voluntary.*)

Tony: I saw some seals on the rocks. I'll show you how they wriggled on their stomachs to get to the water. Then I'll try to show them swimming. My! My! How they could swim! (*He demonstrates. The other children similarly portray activities that they observed or carried out at the beach.*)

This, then, may be the approach in introducing rhythmic interpretation of movements and encouraging dramatic play. In building toward a successful activity, the teacher has (1) given forethought to the objectives of the lesson and the approaches to it; (2) shown the children his enthusiasm for rhythms by demonstrations and thus set a positive tone for subsequent activities; and (3) drawn out the children's thoughts and feelings by discussion and opportunities for dramatic interpretation.

At subsequent sessions, the teacher may wish to vary his approach still further by improvising and chanting verses as the children perform their rhythmic interpretations. Such verses need not rhyme, but should certainly reflect a definite rhythm in keeping with the nature of the movements to be carried out. The verses should also be kept simple and brief so that the children can easily pick them up and repeat them as the performance continues.

Rhythms of Music

Much of the children's rhythmic interpretation can be done to the accompaniment of music. The teacher may play the piano or some other instrument, or play one of the recordings expressly produced for use in the rhythms period of the school day. Also rhythm band instruments can be put to good use as selected pupils manipulate the triangle, cymbals, sand blocks, and drums as an accompaniment to the rhythmic actions of the children who are portraying ponies, elephants, clowns, squirrels, or birds flying before the wind.

Dramatization of Literature

By stages, children advance from simple rhythmic activities and dramatic play based on their personal experiences to the interpretation of stories through dramatization. The first acting out of literary selections may feature short, narrative rhymes.

Interpreting Rhymes and Jingles

For the early stages of learning to dramatize, the Mother Goose rhymes make an abundant and excellent resource, especially as children are likely to be already familiar with so many of them. Typical is the following:

Jack and Jill went up the hill
    To fetch a pail of water.
Jack fell down and broke his crown
    And Jill came tumbling after.

Up Jack got and home did trot
    As fast as he could caper.
He went to bed to mend his head
    In vinegar and brown paper.

What a joyous time for the girl and boy who are giving their impressions of Jill and Jack as the teacher and their classmates recite the verses! Even though a discussion of what Jack and Jill did may precede the acting out, the two characters should give their personal interpretations. All in all, any teacher-led discussion should be most brief, as Jack-and-Jill-in-the-flesh will be more inclined to action than to discourse.

Other Mother Goose rhymes which lend themselves to rhythmic interpretation are the following:

Baa-baa Black Sheep	Little Bopeep
Georgie Porgie	Old King Cole
Humpty-Dumpty	Polly Put the Kettle on
Little Jack Horner	Rock-a-bye Baby
Old Mother Hubbard	Shoe the Horse
Little Miss Muffet	Wee Willie Winkie

Putting on Informal Dramatizations of Stories

Often a reading lesson may close with an extemporaneous dramatization of the story just read. Here there is no preliminary discussion of the characters or action. The children simply assume a part and cooperate with the rest of the "cast" in playing the story. Or, some fluent readers may read aloud as some of the other children pantomime the action. Sometimes, the pantomiming may come first; the audience watch for the action, then select the passages which specifically relate the action that has just been portrayed.

Portions of library books may also be the basis for informal dramatization. Typical of the books that may be used is Robert McCloskey's *Make Way for Ducklings,* in which a policeman halts all the heavy Boston traffic to let a mother duck and her ducklings cross a busy street.

To initiate dramatization of the delightful book, the teacher would hold up a picture of the duck family, all in a row, crossing the street while a burly policeman holds back astonished drivers. Then would ensue a discussion of all that lies back of Mother Duck's desire to get across. Here is a typical dialogue:

> *Mrs. Smiley*:   What do you see happening in this picture?
>
> *Juan*:   A mother duck and her baby ducks are going across the street. A big fat policeman is holding back all the trucks and cars.
>
> *Hattie*:   Don't the drivers look surprised? I think that's an awful funny picture.
>
> *Mrs. Smiley*:   Why would a wild duck be wanting to go across the street? Why is she in the city at all?
>
> *Mark*:   She wants to get into the park where there is water. Many other ducks live in the park.
>
> *Juan*:   I wish we could play this story. I want to be the first little duck in the line. It is fun to waddle like a duck. Just look at me. (*Laughter*)
>
> *Mrs. Smiley*:   What a good duck you make, Juan. Would the rest of you like to play the story? (*Chorus of "Yes, yes! Let's play the story"*)

With such a reaction, the dramatization is ready to launch. The teacher will in this situation be an inconspicuous but supportive participant in the planning of the play. Maintaining the spirit of fun which pervades the story of the duck family, he will help the children visualize the scenes and the characters involved in them as he leads the discussion and interpolates an occasional enlightening remark. The necessary characters and scenes can be plotted on the chalkboard as an aid in perceiving the essential ingredients of the story to be played.

It is possible to have individual tryouts for the different characters in the story to be played; but dividing the class into groups each of which makes up the entire cast and tries out in a scene is possibly more effective with elementary school children. After the several casts have worked out their own inter-

CHARACTER WHEEL

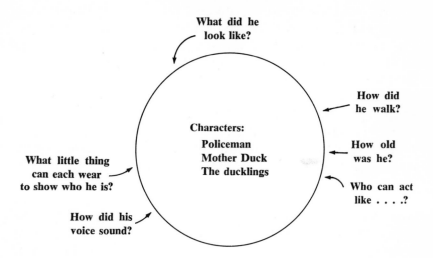

What did he
look like?

How did
he walk?

How old
was he?

What little thing
can each wear
to show who he is?

Characters:
Policeman
Mother Duck
The ducklings

Who can act
like . . . .?

How did his
voice sound?

SCENE WHEEL

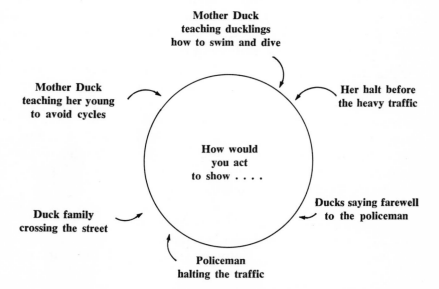

Mother Duck
teaching ducklings
how to swim and dive

Mother Duck
teaching her young
to avoid cycles

Her halt before
the heavy traffic

How would
you act
to show . . . .

Duck family
crossing the street

Ducks saying farewell
to the policeman

Policeman
halting the traffic

pretations of the story, the class as a whole will view and listen so as to make a selection of the portrayal and the cast that have seemed most effective. As with all informal dramatization, the dialogue is improvised by the members of the cast as they follow the general outline of the story. Creativeness and fun lie in the spontaneous actions and ideas which flow from the actors.

Once the dramatization is in progress, the teacher allows the actors to proceed uninterrupted. If there should be a breakdown in continuity of action, the teacher can interject a question or suggestion which will enable the performers to continue. Such comments as may prove necessary should be directed to the action of the story, not to an actor.

In informal dramatization, costumes and scenery are kept to a minimum and, indeed, are usually omitted. There may be a brief discussion of the various locations in the classroom where action will take place. For instance in "The Four Musicians," the players will have to decide where in the classroom is the road the traveling "musicians" are to follow, where the forest and the thieves' hut will be located. However, if a play is to be given before an assembly, a small amount of scenery and very simple costumes may be advisable. Putting the emphasis on creativeness and informal interpretation—and enjoyment—obviates the need for many properties.

Stories to be dramatized by small children should be simple, brief, full of action, and often repetitive as in cumulative tales like "The Gingerbread Man." Tales with familiar characters and action are particularly suitable because the children can easily follow the sequence of the story and give their interpretations of the familiar characters. For the older boys and girls, stories should feature lively adventure and fast action, very dramatic make-believe situations, hero-in-trouble situations, and magical happenings. Following is a list of stories well suited to dramatization.

PRIMARY LEVEL

Ask Mr. Bear (*Marjorie Flack*)

Belling the Cat

Bojabi Tree, The (*Robert Nassau*)

Caps for Sale (*Esphyr Slobodkina*)
Chicken Little
Cinderella
Elves and the Shoemaker, The
Epaminondas
Fairy Shoemaker, The
Ferdinand (*Munro Leaf*)
Five Chinese Brothers (*Claire Bishop*)
Fox and Seven Kids, The
Henny Penny
Just So Stories (*Rudyard Kipling*)
Little Pear (*E. F. Lattimore*)
Little Toot (*Hardie Gramatky*)
Millions of Cats (*Wanda Gag*)

Mother Goose Rhymes
Painted Pig, The (*Elizabeth Morrow*)
Pancake, The
Pelle's New Suit (*Ella Beskow*)
Peter Rabbit (*Beatrix Potter*)
Rumpelstiltskin
Sleeping Beauty, The
Snow White and the Seven Dwarfs
Tar Baby, The (*Joel Chandler Harris*)
Three Bears, The
Three Billy Goats Gruff, The
Three Little Kittens, The
Three Little Pigs, The
Tom Thumb
Wolf and the Seven Little Kids, The

INTERMEDIATE LEVEL

Aladdin
Ali Baba and the Forty Thieves
Bell of Atri, The
Caddie Woodlawn (*Carol Brink*)
500 Hats of Bartholomew Cubbins, The (*Dr. Seuss*)
Golden Touch, The
Hansel and Gretel
Huckleberry Finn (*Mark Twain*)
Johnny Appleseed
Lentil (*Robert McCloskey*)

Penrod (*Booth Tarkington*)
Pinocchio (*Carlo Lorenzini*)
Rapunzel
Robin Hood (various episodes)
Robinson Crusoe (*Daniel Defoe*)
Six Servants, The
Swiss Family Robinson (*Johann Wyss*)
Three Sillies, The
Tom Sawyer (*Mark Twain*)
Treasure Island (*R. L. Stevenson*)

Pantomiming

Stated in the simplest words, pantomime is acting without words. There is much more to pantomiming than mere mute action, for it should express vividly the participants' feelings and thoughts. For example, who cannot interpret fully the wordless actions and facial expression of a boy who is cutting grass on a warm summer day while a baseball game is in progress nearby? In revealing pantomime, the boy heaves a sigh, sweeps his eyes across the uncut expanse of grass to the game across the street and, stolid-faced, resumes his task with feverish haste. By his looks and gestures, he has shown his inner reactions and wordlessly expressed: "I must finish this grass so that I can get over to the ball game."

Introducing Pantomime

The primary teacher is not introducing anything completely new when she gives children an opportunity to pantomime. Children practice it spontaneously every day as they mimic their elders, ride an imaginary horse, zoom in airplane fashion across the yard, or wordlessly enact any of hundreds of pantomimes so natural to them.

There are many ways to introduce pantomiming. Often the opportunity comes without any deliberate planning. One first-grade teacher, for instance, noted a little girl vigorously "sweeping out the kitchen" the day after she had told them the story of Cinderella. Quietly she called the attention of the other girls and boys and asked, "Does Sue remind you of someone in a story I have told you?" Their response came in a chorus of "Cinderella! She is Cinderella!" The teacher continued: "Who can show us something else that Cinderella did? Just show us. Don't talk." From that point on, pantomime became a favorite form of creative expression.

Another teacher used Mother Goose rhymes as a point of departure in pantomiming because of their general popularity and the simple lively verses. One rhyme that worked well was:

> One, two, buckle my shoe;
> Three, four, knock at the door;
> Five, six, pick up sticks;
> Seven, eight, lay them straight. . . .

In introducing the activity, the teacher ran through the rhyme as she demonstrated the actions that might accompany each part. Then she asked the children to give their own interpretations individually as the remainder of the class said the rhyme with her. She was not at all alarmed when some of the pantomimes were "carbon copies" of hers. Eventually the children would come to express their own ideas in their own way.

Later this teacher developed group pantomime from this same rhyme as the children popped up in cumulative style so that one, two, three, four, ... were enacting to correspond to the wording of the rhyme. In all, ten or more children were pantomiming at the end.

Mother Goose rhymes and other simple poems set to music can afford other opportunities for interpreting literature through pantomime. Especially valuable in this connection are those that the children know by rote. One child or a group may pantomime as the teacher and class recite or sing the verses.

Using riddles and guessing games is another delightful way to teach pantomiming to young children. In the game "Who Am I?" the teacher says, "Watch and see who you think I am," as she proceeds to act out the role of a fisherman. Children are eager to guess *who,* then enjoy giving their own impressions of how to fish.

Upper-grade pupils should pantomime without direction if they have engaged in dramatic activities in their progress up the grades. Otherwise, there may be a reluctance on the part of some boys and girls to engage in such activities. In that case, the teacher may give an informal demonstration, preferably of some amusing and humorous situation, such as Jonathan Bing's when he found that he had no hat or tie. Usually the most timid and reserved of children will find such a demonstration "breaks the ice."

Demonstrating How to Pantomime

The teacher's first demonstration of pantomime should be made up of gross actions so that what is being portrayed will be easily recognized by the pupils. Fishing, playing ball, hurrying to answer the telephone are typical, large-movement pantomimes that make suitable beginnings. Upon completing the pantomime, the teacher asks the children to guess the situation and supportive actions that have been enacted. Then they should present their own individual interpretations of this same situation, later to enact some other familiar activities for their classmates to guess. Through constructive discussion, the class can set up standards for an effective pantomime.

Inducing Pupils' Original Pantomime

With these small beginnings of original interpretation, the children should be ready to launch into full-blown pantomime that is completely original. To induce independent action, the teacher may make a chalkboard list of the children's suggestions of possible situations to be portrayed. Each child may then choose an appealing situation, consider privately how to make his portrayal, and present his version for the entertainment of his peers. Children find such activities to be genuine fun, and literature really comes alive as they, individually or as groups, give lifelike reenactments of episodes and characterizations in stories. One excellent activity consists of having a fluent oral reader read a lively story as a selected cast pantomimes the action simultaneously.

At all times, the pantomimes which children give should be simple efforts, devoid of elaborate sets and properties. Only if a concept cannot be made clear without a property should one be used.

As with younger girls and boys, older pupils enjoy the game approach to pantomime. Whether it be called *Charades* or *Secret* or *Who Am I,* it is hilarious fun to try to guess what action is being pantomimed. Often children get the erroneous impression that a pantomime has been well performed if the class has been fooled and no one is able to guess the pantomime. The contrary is true. The mark of an effective pantomime is that it is precisely and clearly presented and that it is easy to identify. It is advisable for the teacher to know in advance just what pantomime a child is going to give. Thus he can avoid any poor taste in choice or performance, and the pantomime-player can be given suggestions that will add to the effectiveness of his performance. The teacher will also be gaining a knowledge of criteria that will guide future performances.

There ultimately comes a day when the teacher feels that the pupils are ready for much more refined portrayal and precise movements. These pantomimes also should be based on actions which are generally familiar and fairly easy to recognize. Here the watchers may be expected to discriminate between somewhat similar actions, such as peeling a banana / peeling an orange, frying a pancake / scrambling eggs, dialing a telephone / pecking on a typewriter, and the like. Youngsters will have a great deal of fun thinking up situations that are somewhat similar, yet demanding of increased finesse in the movements required.

Involving Groups in Pantomiming

A final variation for older pupils is the group pantomime. This is an excellent activity for those children who are somewhat shy about giving individual interpretations, but who get a "kick" out of pantomiming. Groups can be handled in two ways: (1) allow the formation of groups consisting of two or three pupils so that each group can prepare a different pantomime, and (2) have different groups work out the same situation so that comparisons can be made.

In group pantomimes, there often is a tendency for boys to form separate groups and to overemphasize excessively active situations, such as war or athletic sports. This need not be a matter of much concern as literature can be so selected that equally appealing situations of a more refined type can be featured. There are boys who react very sensitively to situations in fiction or biography and are prone to give delicately expressive portrayals of the feelings and ideas of the story characters.

While the quality of pantomimes will depend much upon the individual talents of the pupils and the true cohesiveness of the class group, the teacher's attitudes and leadership are always governing factors. He must give himself wholeheartedly to the enterprise, since a mock effort is quickly recognized as such and the whole enterprise may fall flat. Sincerity and empathy with the children in their characterizations and interpretations of action are essential in teaching pantomime.

Recommended Situations to Pantomime

There follow several lists of situations to be pantomimed. It is hoped that they will be suggestive of scores of other types of actions that can be acted out silently.

SIMPLE PANTOMIMES

Buying a theater ticket	Feeding a dog or cat
Catching a butterfly	Putting on a coat
Drinking water	Setting the table
Suffering from a toothache	Playing catch
Picking roses	Tying a shoelace
Choosing and eating school lunch	Washing dishes

GROUP PANTOMIMES

Two boys giving their dog a bath
A boy asking a girl for his first date
Two girls talking on the telephone
Two adults watching a funny television show
Two boys watching a football game
Playing catch
Mother entering a room as two children try to sneak her present into house

STORY PANTOMIMES

Aladdin seeing the Genie for the first time
Homer Price trying to stop the doughnut machine
Johnny Appleseed spreading the apple seeds
Paul Bunyan chopping down a forest
The Pied Piper leading the children from Hamelin town
Rip Van Winkle awakening from his sleep
Tom Sawyer and friends whitewashing the fence
William Tell shooting the apple from his son's head
Wizard of Oz meeting Dorothy and her friends
Sal and the cub following the wrong mother (*Blueberries for Sal*)
Little Jack Horner and Little Miss Muffet showing what happened
Simple Simon buying something at the fair
Abraham Lincoln rescuing pig from deep mud
Molly Pitcher taking husband's place at the cannon

Puppetry

The educational value of puppetry can scarcely be over-estimated. For the self-conscious child, it affords opportunities to get his mind off himself and on to the "actor" he is manipulating. It tends to improve for all children the correctness of their speech and language usage because boys and girls imitate the standard English which their puppets presumably will be using, and the children want their puppets to do creditably well. Furthermore, puppetry calls for group work wherein the members of a class working on a puppet show pool their creative ideas in designing puppets and preparing script.

The word *puppet* (doll) is an all-inclusive term comprising two types of hand-manipulated, artificial figures. Actually *puppet* refers to a doll that is worked directly by hand, while *marionette* means a doll that is operated by strings. The two types range from the simplest finger, stick and paper-bag puppets for kindergarten and primary grade children to the complex string-operated marionettes for older pupils and for adults. Naturally elementary schools should be concerned mainly with the simple puppets which children can make for themselves and put to immediate use. A discussion of marionettes is beyond the scope of this book.

Preparing for Puppetry

In getting ready to give a puppet show, it is necessary first to decide the story to be presented. Thereupon the children begin to conjure up a mental picture of how each puppet should look and the kind of personality its face and actions will portray. In thinking such matters through, they also consider which is the best type of puppets to use. These matters decided, the puppeteers give thought to the dialogue to be spoken by their hand-manipulated actors.

In selecting a story, the teacher and children should remember that it must be simple, but lively and action-filled. A fast-moving plot is essential because the facial features of the puppets remain constant throughout the play so that ongoing action must suffice to hold the audience's attention. Another reason for the story having to be simple and short is that a maximum limited to three can be operating puppets at one and the same time. Besides, there is a limit to how much dialogue child-puppeteers can carry.

Preparing the Various Types of Puppets

Once the story line and type of puppet have been decided, each character must be given a definite "personality" in the minds of the children. To achieve this, there should be teacher-led discussions and tentative sketches of face and costume for each puppet should be prepared. Sometimes a teacher has in mind the type of puppets that can be used and the steps for the children to follow in making them, only to find that the children cannot cope with the exacting workmanship required. A general rule of thumb is that primary children should construct the simple stick and hand puppets and that the more difficult papier-mâché puppets should be left to older pupils to make.

In directing the children's development of puppets, the teacher must impress on them the importance of facial expressions. The face is focal, since the body is relatively immobile and lacks individuality. The pupils must be helped to build "character" into the eyes, nose, mouth, facial contours, and hair.

The stick puppet is the easiest one to make and is suitable for use with children as young as kindergartners. In constructing one, the outlined figure is usually drawn on a piece of lightweight construction paper or oaktag. This figure is then pasted on a piece of cardboard, cut out and mounted on a stick (a dowel rod or lathing will do) by means of a thumbtack. Once this is done, it can be colored or painted to fit the character of the puppet. Arms and legs, trunks and tails on animals, and other movable parts can be appended by using brass fasteners or by attaching wires to them and then fastening them to the stick.

Another group of puppets relatively easy to make is the so-called hand puppet, which can be fashioned from almost every conceivable kind of material, many of them cheap and immediately at hand in the American household. Here is a representative list:

apple	light bulbs	spongex
carrot	potato	styrofoam
cotton-stuffed sock	rag doll head	socks
darning "egg"	rubber ball	turnip
gourds	soap	yam

The simplest type of hand puppet from the standpoint of materials and construction is the paper-bag puppet. For this one uses a relatively small paper bag whose corners at its bottom are stapled to make the bag round. It is then turned inside out and stuffed to make a head. A round tube (toilet tissue cores work well) is inserted into the bag and a neckline is made by drawing a string around the tube below the head. Holes are then cut into the sides of the bag to accommodate the thumb and middle finger of the child. Now the puppet head and body are ready to have the facial features and "costume" painted on.

The papier-mâché puppet is popular, though considerably more difficult for children to make. Its head is made first by fashioning newspaper pulp mixed with wheat paste around the top of a small cylinder. To this mass is applied torn strips of newsprint soaked in the paste solution, one strip being added at a time. After several layers have formed a substantial foundation, the resulting egg-shaped head can be molded to form facial features which reflect the desired "character." After this is dry, it is painted and shellacked.

The puppet-makers may desire to make the puppet's facial features more clearly defined. For instance, eyes and nose can be made from buttons, thumbtacks or marbles pressed into the soft mass at the time of the molding. A mouth can be represented by attaching cutout paper or using pushpins packed closely together. Hair may be made from any number of kinds of material, among which are cotton, rope, string or yarn; shredded paper and toweling; steel wool; and wood shavings.

The body of the papier-mâché puppet consists of the palm and wrist of the puppeteer which are hidden by pieces of clothing fastened to the neck (cardboard tube) by tacks, wire, or string. This garment should be a simple one representative of the character of the puppet. Hands held on by wire can protrude from the sleeves, and stuffed socks can be sewed to the lower garment to represent feet. In all, the costume should be long enough to cover the hand of the puppeteer, and the sleeves broad enough to admit his fingers. When not in use, the puppet should be kept clean by storing in a cardboard box.

Staging a Puppet Show

The stage and staging of a puppet show should be as simple as possible. A long table turned on its side or turned upside down is an easily arranged stage for displaying the puppets while concealing the manipulators. On the overturned table, a curtain is stretched from leg to leg and supported by a window pole. Large appliance boxes make workable stages too, with the upper half of the front of the box being cut back to show the puppets, and the lower half at the back also being cut out so that the puppeteers can enter from the rear. If large appliance boxes are used, there should be some type of anchor weight that will prevent them from tipping over.

To improve the staging, the appliance box can be decorated, both inside and out, with Christmas tree bulbs as a source of lighting. Other than giving these slight touches, properties should be few and restricted to any that are absolutely necessary. In the story, "The Princess and the Pea," for example, a few mattresses (pieces of cloth) will be needed, but all other items should be painted on the inside of the stage or on a backdrop.

Manipulation of the Puppets

Manipulating puppets is not an easy job, but the children can learn to follow a few ground rules. Since it is difficult to speak lines and to manipulate a puppet at the same time, the child puppeteers should run through a play once or twice before presenting it in front of an audience. Pupils who are fluent and resourceful may well improvise as they go along after they are sure of the story to be portrayed; less gifted children may need to rehearse definitely preplanned dialogue. Children should be given plenty of time to practice in the manipulation of puppets until they become skillful at it. They should also try out different voice qualities so as to be able to use the pitch and quality that suggests a fairy or elf, a witch, a giant, a puppy, a mastiff, an elderly person, or a child.

Possible Stories to Be Shown Through Using Puppets

The stories suitable for puppet plays are legion, since a story that can be presented through other types of dramatic activities may be adapted for puppetry—assuming that there are no more than three characters performing simultaneously. Here are a few particularly good stories:

PRIMARY	INTERMEDIATE
Mother Goose rhymes	Aladdin
The Three Bears	Homer Price
The Three Billy Goats Gruff	King of the Golden River
Little Red Riding Hood	Robin Hood
Snipp, Snapp, and Snurr	Treasure Island

Children should be encouraged to write original stories and to adapt them for puppetry. A group or class working together may develop excellent puppet plays from the incidents of history, customs shown in human geography, and health practices as these come up in their lessons.

Formal Play Production

Formal play production at the elementary school level is often disparaged because long hours of rehearsal are required, because suitable scripts are lacking, and because pupils should not experience the tedium of forced memorization. Instead of abandoning the idea of producing formal plays, however, teachers may consider the needs and capabilities of the children and work out some finished performances for the more mature and gifted ones, for there is good to be found in the experience of participating in a play that is a polished performance.

The major responsibility of "producing" a play at the elementary school level falls upon the classroom teacher. This he must assume if he genuinely feels a desire to give his pupils such an experience which will result in real learning.

Steps in Play Production

The first step in producing is to make the selection of the play, which can be done in a number of ways. The teacher may turn to some publication as *Plays* or *The Instructor* or to a book of plays, such as those listed in the bibliography. Or he may, in cooperation with a music instructor, locate an operetta or other type of dramatic musical production. A more creative approach involves cooperative endeavor of the teacher and his pupils in selecting a story which they can adapt into a play that they will write for themselves.

Whatever the situation, the chief responsibility for selecting a play falls upon the classroom teacher. It is he who best knows the children, and can identify a vehicle which will most adequately fit their needs and meet their interests. Knowing their limitations, he can eliminate any play which requires maturity or a particular talent which is missing in his group of pupils. Finally he must consider the problems of costuming and staging and avoid any play for which costuming and staging demands are insuperable. Any teacher experienced in producing plays knows how difficult such problems can be.

Once the play has been selected, the teacher must go over it with the children, devoting particular care and thoroughness to any play they have not written for themselves. At first he presents only the highlights of the plot and points out, for example, how well the play fits into what is currently being studied, or how appropriate it is for this particular season of the year. Most children "go for" the idea of giving a formal play and are ready to hear about it in general detail.

Next, the teacher introduces the story of the play in considerable detail. This he may do by distributing printed copies of a commercially published play or mimeographed copies of one taken from a magazine or written by the pupils. As the children watch, he reads the entire script to them orally, after which he is usually flooded with suggestions for ways of improving the play. Those that are constructive and feasible should by all means be utilized. Allowing such suggestions is one way of retaining creative qualities in a formal production.

At this point, the teacher must make a fundamental decision: how to select pupils to play the various roles. Shall he decide this matter for himself? Should he have formal tryouts by individuals and/or groups who compete for the roles? Should he have the children vote on the cast? Some teachers prefer to make a careful match of role with actor, so making sure that each part will be acted by the boy or girl best fitted to act it. Generally speaking, children accept the teacher's decisions, especially if he gives his reasons for selecting various pupils for particular roles when he announces his choices.

On the one hand, allowing children to try out for parts in a play often establishes it as their own and, in the process, the pupils may give some very creative impersonations and interpretations—ideas that may not have occurred to the teacher. On the other hand, having the pupils vote on who is to play a particular role can result in a popularity contest instead of a talent search. Even so, the children can be so carefully directed that they do consider carefully the aptitudes of their peers and make their selections with insight and good judgment. All in all, if time permits, tryouts are to be preferred, for children can actually be good judges of who best fits each part in a formalized play.

Rehearsals

The cast having been decided, practice should begin. Under all circumstances, plays should be practiced during school hours. Occasionally a youngster who has the lead in the play or who needs some special coaching may stay a short time after school if doing so seems absolutely necessary and if parents, child, and teacher agree that it is to be done.

In preparing for rehearsals, some teacher-directors like to plot out beforehand the stage settings for a formal play. These he may register in a prompter's book or he may draw them to scale on diagrams of the stage. However, doing this may take time and effort that the teacher cannot afford. There is probably more learning value in the procedure of deciding on the stage settings through a discussion with the class or through decision by a committee of pupils set up by the class.

Copies of the play having been distributed to the cast, there is a read-through of the lines, followed by a walk-through to demonstrate the staging as each character performs. In this initial stage, the teacher accents the gross actions, positioning, matching up of dialogue and movement, and the sequence of action. In the walk-through, the actors may or may not have copies of the play in their hands. Many teachers prefer to work without the copies and to put the words into the children's mouths as they go "through their paces" for the first time. This is because a child with a paper before him tends to concentrate on the lines and to be oblivious of the actions he must learn to perform.

All the while the actors should be committing the dialogue to memory. At the same time, the teacher must be working diligently *with* them on their interpretation of their roles and the characters they are to represent. The importance of his doing this cannot be overemphasized. Lack of knowledge of how to say his lines, or a singsong rendition of lines, or inability to represent the traits and feelings of the character being portrayed can lead to poor ways of interpreting dialogue and the children can develop extremely bad habits hard to overcome. The teacher-director, in order to get the children to understand the characters, will repeatedly stop the action and ask such questions as "How does Cinderella feel when she is saying that line?" "How can you better show that feeling?" "What are you supposed to be doing with that lantern?"

Any teacher with considerable training and knowledgeability in acting techniques may tend to insist on too much detail in the finer points of acting. Doing this can prove "fatal" when working with elementary school children. It will "kill" the play. Pupils should be held to only a few major points of technique if the production is not to bog down in minutiae. Among the important rules for elementary school actors are—

1. Avoid looking at any one particular person in the audience.
2. Always face toward the front of the stage.
3. Stand or sit still when you or someone else is speaking a line.
4. Wait during laughs and applause.
5. As a cast, keep in mind the fact that you should distribute yourselves in natural groups and utilize the total stage area.
6. If you forget a line, do not panic. Listen to the prompter.

A day or two prior to the final presentation of the play, there should be two rehearsals, one devoted to a review of the lines only, the other to lines *and* movements. One rehearsal should be a dress rehearsal if costumes are to be used. It is important that the teacher-director not stop the actors as they recite their lines during the final rehearsals, although he may find it advisable to make some suggestions for improvement at the end of the rehearsal period.

Stage Management

Behind-the-scene preparation is all important to the success of a play production. It may be that more effort and time are expended here than in the rehearsals as such. Fortunately, pupils can assume much responsibility in this area; for instance,

1. A reliable, highly resourceful boy or girl should be appointed as stage manager. This child, who could easily carry one of the major roles in the play, should be made to realize that stage managership is a key job—possibly more than equivalent to a part in the play.
2. A clear-voiced boy or girl should serve as prompter and, if need be, as narrator.
3. As far as practicable, the children should prepare or provide the sets and properties.

4. The class should design and distribute the invitations and programs for the play.
5. If costumes are to be used, the help of parents should be solicited, each parent providing for his own child so far as possible.
6. Avoid or minimize the use of makeup.

Selected Readings for Creative Dramatics

Books for Young People

EMBERLEY, ED. *Punch & Judy: A Play for Puppets.* Boston: Little, Brown, 1965.

FULLER, EDMUND. *A Pageant of the Theatre.* New York: T. Y. Crowell, 1965.

GRAYSON, MARION. *Let's Do Fingerplays.* Washington, D.C.: Luce, 1962.

HELFMAN, HARRY. *Tricks With Your Fingers.* New York: Morrow, 1967.

HELFMAN, HARRY AND ELIZABETH. *Strings On Your Fingers: How to Make String Figures.* New York: Morrow, 1967.

HIRSCHFELD, BURT. *Stagestruck: Your Career in Theatre.* New York: Messner, 1963.

HODGES, CYRIL. *Shakespeare's Theatre.* New York: Coward, 1964.

HOWARD, VERNON. *Pantomimes, Charades and Skits.* New York: Sterling, 1967.

————. *Puppet and Pantomime Plays.* New York: Sterling, 1967.

HUNT, DOUGLAS AND KARI. *Pantomime: The Silent Theater.* New York: Atheneum, 1964.

HUNT, KARI, AND CARLSON, BERNICE. *Masks and Mask Makers.* Nashville: Abingdon Press, 1961.

JAGENDORF, MORITZ. *Penny Puppets, Penny Theatre, and Penny Plays.* Boston: Plays, Inc., 1966.

SCHWON, KARL. *The First Book of Acting.* New York: Watts, 1965.

SMITH, MOYNE. *Plays and How to Put Them On.* New York: Walck, 1961.

VANCE, MARGUERITE. *Hear the Distant Applause: Six Great Ladies of the American Theatre.* New York: Dutton, 1963.

WAGNER, FREDERICK, AND BRADY, BARBARA. *Famous American Actors and Actresses.* New York: Dodd, 1961.

WYNDHAM, LEE. *Acting, Acting, Acting.* New York: Watts, 1962.

Collections of Plays

BIRNER, WILLIAM. *Twenty Plays for Young People: A Collection of Plays for Children.* Anchorage, Ky.: Anchorage, 1967.

BOLOGNESE, DON. *Plays &—How to Put Them On.* New York: Walck, 1961.

DE ANGELI, ARTHUR. *The Door In The Wall: A Play.* Garden City, N.Y.: Doubleday, 1968.

DIAS, EARL. *New Comedies for Teen-Agers: A Collection of One-Act, Royalty-Free Comedies, Farces, and Melodramas.* Boston: Plays, Inc., 1967.

DURRELL, DONALD, AND CROSSLEY, B. A. *Thirty Plays for Classroom Reading: A New Approach to the Reading Program in the Intermediate Grades.* Boston: Plays, Inc., 1968.

FENNER, PHYLLIS, AND HUGHES, AVAH. *Entrances and Exits: A Book of Plays for Young Actors.* New York: Dodd, 1960.

HOWARD, VERNON. *The Complete Book of Children's Theater.* New York: Doubleday, 1969.

JARVIS, SALLY. *Fried Onions and Marshmallows, and Other Little Plays for Little People.* New York: Parents, 1968.

KAMERMAN, SYLVIA. *Fifty Plays for Children.* Boston: Plays, Inc., 1969.

LILLINGTON, KENNETH. *The Second Book of Classroom Plays.* London: R. Hale, 1968.

MILLER, HELEN. *Short Plays for Children: A Collection of Royalty-Free Comedies, Mysteries, Folk Tales and Holiday Plays for Boys and Girls.* Boston: Plays, Inc., 1969.

SMITH, MOYNE. *Seven Plays & How to Produce Them.* New York: Walck, 1968.

THANE, ADELE. *Plays from Famous Stories and Fairy Tales: Royalty-Free Dramatizations of Favorite Children's Stories.* Boston: Plays, Inc., 1967.

WEIK, MARY. *The Scarlet Thread.* New York: Atheneum, 1968.

Creative and Formal Dramatics: Teacher References

BURGER, ISABEL. *Creative Play Acting: Learning Through Drama.* New York: Ronald, 1966.

CHILVER, PETER. *Stories for Improvisation in Primary and Secondary Schools.* London: Batsford, 1969.

COURTS, ANN. *Teaching Language Arts Creatively.* Minneapolis: T. S. Denison, 1965.

DAVIS, JED, AND WATKINS, MARY JANE. *Children's Theatre: Play Production for the Child Audience.* New York: Harper, 1960.

FIDELL, ESTELLE. *Play Index, 1961-1967: an Index to 4,793 Plays.* New York: Wilson, 1968.

FORKERT, OTTO. *Children's Theatre . . . . That Captures Its Audience.* Chicago: Coach Hse., 1962.

HAKE, HERBERT. *Here's How.* New York: French, 1965.

HUCKLEBERRY, ALAN, AND STROTHER, EDWARD. *Speech Education for the Elementary Teacher.* Boston: Allyn, 1966.

Humpty Dumpty Magazine. "Little Plays for Little People." New York: Parents, 1965.

KASE, C. ROBERT. *Stories for Creative Acting.* New York: French, 1965.

MCCASLIN, NELLIE. *Creative Dramatics in the Classroom.* New York: McKay, 1968.

SCHATTNER, REGINA. *Creative Dramatics for Handicapped Children.* New York: John Day, 1967.

SIKS, GERALDINE, AND DUNNINGTON, HAZEL. *Children's Theatre and Creative Dramatics.* Seattle: U. of Wash. Pr., 1967

SIKS, GERALDINE. *Children's Literature for Dramatization: An Anthology.* New York: Harper & Row, 1964.

TAYLOR, LOREN. *Formal Drama and Children's Theatre.* Minneapolis: Burgess, 1966.

————. *Storytelling and Dramatization.* Minneapolis: Burgess, 1965.

Puppetry: Teacher References

ADAIR, MARGARET. *Do It in a Day: Puppets for Beginners.* New York: John Day, 1964.

BAINBRIDGE, CECIL. *Hand Puppets.* New Rochelle, N.Y.: Soccer Associates, 1968.

BAIRD, BIL. *The Art of the Puppet.* Boston: Plays, Inc., 1965.

BLACKMAN, OLIVE. *Shadow Puppets.* New York: Harper & Row, 1960.

BRAMALL, ERIC. *Puppet Plays and Playwriting.* London: G. Bell and Sons, 1961.

BRAMALL, ERIC, AND SOMERVILLE, CHRISTOPHER. *Expert Puppet Techniques.* London: Faber & Faber, 1963.

BURGIN, NORMA. *Let's Look at Puppets.* Racine, Wis.: Whitman Pub., 1967.

CUMMINGS, RICHARD. *101 Hand Puppets: A Guide for Puppeters of All Ages.* New York: McKay, 1962.

JONES, JOSEPHINE. *Glove Puppetry.* London: English Universities Press, 1961.

LEWIS, SHARI. *Making Easy Puppets.* New York: Dutton, 1967.

MULHOLLAND, JOHN. *Practical Puppetry.* New York: Arco, 1961.

NELSON, LESLIE. *Instructional Aids.* 2nd ed. Dubuque, Iowa: Wm. C. Brown, 1970.

PHILPOTT, ALEXIS. *Eight Plays for Hand Puppets.* Boston: Plays, Inc., 1968.

ROSS, LAURA. *Hand Puppets: How to Make and Use Them.* New York: Lothrop, 1969.

TAYLOR, LOREN. *Puppetry, Marionettes and Shadow Plays.* Minneapolis: Burgess, 1965.

CHAPTER
5

Storytelling

Among all of the skills of communication, history has known none that has brought greater pleasure to children and adults alike than the skillful telling of stories. Our records of earliest civilizations—cave drawings, hieroglyphs, pictographs —reveal that stories have been an integral part of peoples' lives throughout the ages. Remnants of these stories are found today in the folktales, the myths, the legends, and the hero tales that are a part of every culture. In fact, some of the clearest interpretations we have of early peoples are found in those stories that were passed from father to son; the accretions of each generation can be detected. The storyteller, in communicating a favorite tale, has woven his imaginings and his perceptions into that tale and passed it along as additional evidence of how his people laughed and sorrowed and struggled, how they dreamed and hoped and despaired.

As we consider storytelling, we discover two important principles. The first is that children are naturally good storytellers, and we are indeed remiss if we do not provide them opportunities to develop that skill. A story that got into print is always restricting; the reading book communicates only those ideas that appear there. On the other hand, the storyteller can take a familiar tale and weave it skillfully, adding threads from his own imagination that will give the story special appeal for his audience of the moment. The creative child elaborates on a simple theme, expanding it according to his images and his perceptions. As he captures the interest of his audience, he tends to develop real pride in his powers of communication and in his ability to give pleasure to others.

Second, a story never really lives until it is told and heard by someone. Because of limited family and neighborhood experiences, many children have never discovered the real thrill of a story that is skillfully told. As they gather with their teacher and their playmates in school, they experience the unfolding of a world of wonder—a world of there and then which transcends the here and now of their daily living. In contrast to listening to a ready-made, already written story which is necessarily limited in scope, the child is listening to the teacher-teller of stories at a level far above that of most written materials. Using rich and vibrant language, the teacher can help the listeners to become increasingly aware of intriguing words and equally intriguing ideas.

The Teacher as a Storyteller

Too many teachers turn to the book for relating the fascinating world of children's literature. There is a measure of security in being able to read a well-written story, and reading aloud to children requires real skill. However, nothing compares to sitting down with an audience of children and unfolding a story that is communicated with no barrier between children and storyteller. The storyteller is free to use his hands for gestures that may convey more than words ever could; he has utmost freedom in elaborating on a story as long as the audience is interested. Further, the continuous eye contact that the storyteller maintains with his audience is an improtant factor in awakening and holding interest.

Anyone can tell a story, but not all stories should be told. Some were written to be read exactly as written. It would be very difficult, for example, to tell the story of *Thidwick the Big Hearted Moose*, or any other story written by Dr. Seuss. The author's rare choice of words, his sense of timing and rhythm, are difficult to relate unless one reads the story. This is to say that the teacher must know how to select stories which she is to read or to tell to children. She must know the sources of all types of stories for each audience, for each occasion. Her repertoire of stories may range from simple folktales that can be told in three or four minutes to elaborate mysteries of hero tales that require a half hour for telling. At the end of this chapter we have suggested sources of stories for the teacher and for the children.

The skills for telling a good story are the same for all persons. It is inconceivable that any teacher would dislike telling stories or that she might not seize every opportunity for sharing a good story with children. Any teacher can become a good storyteller with practice—plus a little enthusiasm and determination.

Creating an Atmosphere

Whenever a teacher or child prepares to tell a story in the classroom, care should be taken to create an atmosphere of quiet and anticipated enjoyment among the listeners. There is nothing more disconcerting to the person who has taken the care to prepare a story than to attempt to tell that story to a wriggling, noisy audience. In all language activities, the teacher should discuss with children the values and pleasure to be gained from careful, polite listening. She can quickly set the stage for storytelling by asking children to remove all materials from their desks and to sit quietly while she tells the story. Good listening requires the attention of the entire body; if the child is toying with a pencil, crayons, or papers on his desk, he is certain to be dividing his attention.

If the first story that a teacher tells to a group of children is a good one, and the children feel that they have been rewarded for giving full attention, then the next storytelling session will be easier. There is nothing quite so infectious as the pleasure the teacher herself feels as she tells her story. If the experience has been a satisfying and exciting one, a warm relationship between the storyteller and the listeners can be established—a relationship that may last through untold numbers of happy story hours throughout the year.

Many teachers are concerned about whether they should attempt to tell stories to a total class, since they believe that storytelling in small groups is more effective. A good storyteller may be master of a large audience, and there are many occasions when the entire class will enjoy listening together.

As children become adept at telling stories, they should be encouraged to tell a favorite story in a small group.

Developing Skill as a Storyteller

Nothing can be substituted for skill. One may love good literature, know hundreds of good stories, and have a burning desire to tell those stories, but if the storyteller neglects to learn the essentials of good storytelling, he may not maintain his audience.

In the beginning, it is advisable to introduce a few guidelines for helping children learn to become better storytellers. One guideline at a time, consciously followed and practiced, generally results in considerable improvement. As children learn the essential skills, they may become critical of the skills of others. The teacher plays a key role in guiding evaluation of those skills and helps the children to offer constructive criticism and to apply that criticism to their own storytelling.

Select Your Story Carefully

The storyteller will select a story that he is confident he can bring to life. It will be one that he likes so well that he feels he simply must tell it to others. He must know it so well that he can communicate it freely, without taking recourse to notes or pausing to remember details.

People of the same age group are likely to have different interests. Hence, it is not always wise to suggest that a certain story will invariably appeal to all children of a particular age group. Some will respond enthusiastically to fantasy; others will thrill at a real-life experience involving older people. Some are in need of relaxation and fun. The storyteller is challenged to choose a story that has special appeal for his current listening audience.

Appropriateness is the key to selection of stories for particular groups of children, both in terms of the ages of the children and the seasonal appeal of the story. Children in kindergarten appear to prefer stories of familiar things and people, stories with much repetition of rhythmic phrases or jingles, and stories that move quickly through a simple plot. Older children in the primary grades respond readily to fairy tales, stories of wonder and curiosity. They like to learn the *how* and *why* of the world around them. They respond to the ridiculous and the not-so-true. Kipling's "Elephant's Child" is a favorite; it has the elements of wonder and curiosity, with a generous sprinkling of the ridiculous.

For children of the middle grades, the world of realism and heroic endeavors is emerging. It is a world filled with real-life adventures and heroes. Consequently, stories of adult life, of biography and historical narrative, and of the great epics have the greatest appeal. Paul Bunyan and Pecos Bill; King Arthur and Paul Revere; Helen Keller and Jenny Lind; Robin Hood, Bambi and Heidi are chosen again and again by boys and girls alike.

Too frequently storytelling for the adolescent boy or girl is neglected. We feel that the older children have outgrown storytelling, but nothing could be further from the truth. It is during these years that young people learn to become really skillful tellers of stories. Their activities in camps, schools, churches, and neighborhood groups call for frequent displays of leadership and entertainment. They are often given responsibilities for groups of younger children, and the adolescent who can tell stories is indeed in demand. Further, children of this age group seek perfection of their skills, and storytelling provides another outlet in their search for activities demanding skill.

Adolescence is a distinct period of emerging idealism. These young people are challenged by stories of great men and women who have sacrificed their lives for a principle; they want to believe in unselfish love and flawless character. Their interest in the opposite sex is awakening, and they respond to stories of tender love. It is no chance quirk of fate that *North to the Orient, Invincible Louisa, Call of the Wild, Johnny Tremaine,* and *Thirty Seconds Over Tokyo* remain at the top of the list of best-loved stories for this age group.

It seems obvious that stories should be selected for their appropriateness to the season. Some stories manifestly are appropriate at any time of the year; but there is nothing that can engender excitement more readily about Hallowe'en, Thanksgiving, and Christmas than a good story. "Burg's Hill's On Fire" has all of the ingredients of a good Hallowe'en story—mystery, wonder, and fantasy; and "Why the Chimes Rang" remains a favorite of children of all ages at Christmas time. Further, what could be more appropriate than to say, on a snowy, wintery day, "Once, on a day that must have been just like this one . . . ." There are hundreds of stories that are appropriate for the seasons and for holidays.

Know Your Story Well

Nothing kills a good story so effectively as the person who forgets, transposes the sequence of events, or pauses frequently to recall painfully the details surrounding a critical event in the story. The storyteller must know his story so well that he, in a sense, becomes a part of the story itself.

How, then, does one learn a story well? First, it must be read several times, until the flow of incidents, the characters, and each mental picture, are vivid in the reader's mind. Then, it is advisable to set the story aside and to think it through, incident by incident. If your story is to live for others, it must first be alive for you. Study the characters and their words. Are their exact words necessary for accurate telling of the story? Check the sequence of events. What came first, next, next, last? Finally, translate the story into your *own* words; only then has it become *your* story. If you find that you must refer to note cards, an outline, or a book, select another story —one that you really can master and tell fluently with verve.

Introduce Your Story Carefully

There is a tendency on the part of many storytellers to provide so elaborate an introduction that nothing remains to be told. We all know the person who prefaces his stories with such expressions as, "Say, I have the funniest story you've ever heard," or "This is the story you'll really like." Such a storyteller may have difficulty in proving his preface!

Lead naturally into your story. A story worth telling is worth getting on with; the story's the thing! Relate the story simply to the experiences of your audience. For instance, with the "Blue Pitcher" which appears at the end of this chapter, we have found that an appropriate introduction for primary children goes something like this: "I imagine that everyone here has, at some time or other, broken his promise to someone, such as not doing the work you promised to do, or taking something you had promised you wouldn't. And I imagine you've wondered, when you broke your promise, just how you were going to set things straight again. Well, that's just exactly what happened to Janie. . . ."

Not all stories can begin with "Once upon a time. . . ." Certainly there are many that should start with that time-worn introduction; they are stories of no definite time or place. "Once there was and was not a poor peasant" is a wonderful beginning for the story of "Where One Is Fed a Hundred Can Dine." An appropriate beginning for "Ask Mr. Bear" might be, "Have you ever known a time when you simply couldn't find an answer to your problem and had to go to someone else for help? Let's listen to find out how Bennie found the answer to what he should give his mother for her birthday, when he had no money and couldn't think of anything—not a single thing—to give her." You're into your story with a simple but appropriate introduction.

Pace Your Story

Some stories require a measured cadence; others are told trippingly. Some stories are ponderous and move clumsily; still others emerge hesitantly. Pacing your story is one of the most important essentials. Study your story carefully to determine those places where a pause would be effective. Develop an appreciation for the effect of a crescendo, in both time and intensity.

"Why the Chimes Rang" is an example of a story that moves with measured, majestic cadence, but the story of "Tar Baby" demands an erratic pace. The opening paragraphs of the "Blue Pitcher" should be narrated slowly, because they tell of a little girl who is bored and steeped in lethargy. However, when the Elf Man appears, the pace quickens, and there is a gradual crescendo as Janie and the Elf Man leave the house and reach the land of the bluebells and the fairies. Now the tempo is at a fever-pitch as the fairies work at producing the new pitcher. When Janie turns to thank the fairies, there is a dramatic pause—the fairies have disappeared! Quickly Janie and the Elf Man return to the house. Gently, they place the pitcher on the shelf; slowly, Janie turns from admiring the pitcher to thank the Elf Man for his help. In a frenzy she searches for him in the house and in the garden. And the story ends on a quiet, measured cadence.

Use Your Voice Effectively

A most important ingredient in storytelling is the voice of the storyteller. He may use no gestures and few facial expressions; it is his voice that carries the story.

The beginner must learn to listen to his own voice. He must not be afraid to experiment with it until he achieves the quality that the story demands: laughter, reverence, anger, fear, astonishment, wonder, sorrow. The little Elf Man in the "Blue Pitcher" is frequently impatient, occasionally sharp with Janie. There are times, however, when he is almost tender with this child who is in trouble. How important it is that the voice of the storyteller communicate the shifting of the Elf Man's moods to the listening audience.

Developing and using an appropriate voice for a bear, a small child, a little old women, or an alligator require practice and careful attention to characters and mood in the story. The storyteller works for naturalness and relaxation in his voice; neither is achieved easily, but each is worth working for since it heightens the effectiveness of the story.

The storyteller should work toward the clearest articulation possible, with free and distinct pronunciation of each word. He must guard against stilted, labored articulation which may divert the listeners' attention from the story to the voice.

Select Words Carefully

Sometimes we have a tendency to "talk down" to children when we tell stories to them. We forget that children have lived for several years in a world of adult conversations and that they are capable of listening at a level considerably higher than their measured speaking or reading vocabularies. On the other hand, there is always the danger of talking "over the heads" of children. Finding the magic point between these two extremes, in the selection of appropriate words for our story, is indeed critical. The person who is limited in ideas and imagination is also limited in the use of words. In telling your story, select vivid, colorful, meaningful words; avoid unduly flowery wording and lengthy descriptions or explanations. As we have pointed out before, if you know your story, if it is alive for you, it should flow easily.

Frequently, it is advisable to memorize the exact words of the author to make the story effective. There's sheer magic for the small child in "I'll huff and I'll puff and I'll blow your house in!" and on the second telling of the story, we find the children chiming in, "I'll huff and I'll puff. . . ." Consider the appeal of "the great grey green greasy Limpopo, all surrounded by fever trees," found in the "Elephant's Child." To fail to memorize those words is to fail to communicate much of the charm of the story.

A word of caution regarding dialect should, perhaps, be offered. Few children can handle dialect effectively, and not many adults use it well, either. It's a rare storyteller who can tell the stories of Uncle Remus in the original dialect. The inexperienced person would do much better if he were to tell the stories in his own words and his natural dialect.

Use Gestures Sparingly

Nothing can be more distracting to the listener than stilted, artificial gestures employed by the storyteller. Gestures can, on many occasions, communicate more meaning than words themselves, but they should be used sparingly—only as they actually add to the impact of the passage being read. As you observe professional storytellers, you may be impressed by how infrequently they use their hands. But the storyteller's face is alive with facial "gestures." His mouth, his eyes, his eyebrows communicate sadness, shock, shame, joy, and you are aware of the fact that he uses one of his rare gestures and a facile facial expression because he is internally living the story and is reacting with pure spontaneity and very naturally.

Children frequently feel compelled to use gestures. Encourage the child to tell his story with his hands folded in his lap, lifting them only when necessary to illustrate, to point, or to emphasize.

Sit Naturally and Comfortably

Many storytellers prefer to sit down while they are telling their stories. If standing, they tend to pace or move so much that their movements are distracting to the listeners. Some storytellers sit on the floor, with the children gathered around them; others prefer to sit on a stool, with their knees drawn up comfortably. Whatever you yourself select as a comfortable position, relax and enjoy your storytelling. On the other hand, if your story is dull and unplanned, teeter on the edge of your desk, and swing your feet violently; the distraction may save the day! Perish the thought!

Select a Good Ending for Your Story

Just as we stated about the beginnings of stories, there is frequently a tendency among storytellers to prolong their endings. Instead of ending the story dramatically and finally, they find themselves dragging out the climax or recapitulating the story. If it has been a story well told, no further explanations are necessary. The story should be complete, in and of itself.

Some stories end with a simple statement of fact. "From that day on, Our Lady of Cluny has always smiled." "And there he stands to this day, a pack on his back and a dog at his heels." Some stories are effectively closed with a question, such as the ending of the "Blue Pitcher": "And to this day, Janie doesn't know whether to believe this story or not. I'm not at all sure that I do. Do you?"

Sometimes children will want to discuss a story. However, it is sheer folly to force discussion of a tender story that deserves time and quiet for assimilation and reflection. It is neither necessary nor advisable to prepare a set of questions to be asked at the end of a story. Allow questions to arise spontaneously from the audience, if at all. If a story is told to illustrate a moral or an eternal truth, however, the teacher must be prepared to question the children to determine whether the point was achieved or not. It is important, we believe, that children be allowed to express honest opinions on stories. If they did not like a story, or if they reacted negatively to parts of it, they should be encouraged to state their opinions and reasons. Asking a question such as "Did you like this story?" opens the door for an embarrassing negative rejoinder or may perhaps force an insincere positive response.

Illustrate and Dramatize Stories Occasionally

On occasion, a story can be effectively illustrated by making chalk sketches, using the flannel board, or judiciously presenting an illustration from the book. There is a danger, however, that all of these may detract from the story itself. Some stories were written to be illustrated; for example, "The Tired Lady" is a wonderful story for the flannel board, and the repeated line ". . . but still she sat and still she spun and how she wished her work was done" gives the storyteller an opportunity to move smoothly from one illustration to the next.

The effective storyteller does not need illustrations to tell a story well; the story, the voice, and the pacing do the job sufficiently. The story that is told without illustrations leaves the child with complete freedom to create his own images—images woven from the words of the story itself.

Dramatization and storytelling are obviously closely related activities, and children of all ages enjoy dramatizing a well-known, well-loved story. The important factor in dramatization is thorough familiarization with the story: incidents, sequence, characters, and expressions. However, there may be danger that overuse of dramatization may dampen the desire to tell or read stories. Not all stories can be or should be dramatized. On the other hand, what's more fun than watching children in the kindergarten and first grade as they indulge in histrionics with "The Three Billy Goats Gruff"?

Conclusion

Ruth Sawyer, one of the great storytellers of our time, has given us our conclusion to this discussion of the art of storytelling in her book, *The Way of the Storyteller:*

There is one fact about storytelling that must, like time, be taken by the forelock if there is to be intelligent as well as emotional satisfaction in becoming a storyteller. First must come a clear understanding of what storytelling is and what it is not. I know of so many who go stumbling along with little or no conception of what it is all about. They may be extremely successful at telling some stories, and extremely dreary at telling others. They have never made themselves think. They have liked to tell stories; and no one has kept them from it. This seems to have been all that mattered. It is far easier to dabble than to make oneself think through to some purpose, to comprehend the nature and demands laid upon one when one undertakes an art. . . .

Resources for Storytelling

The following collections of stories are arranged in two groups for the convenience of the teacher. The first group lists collections of stories for the storyteller. The second group refers to standard references about storytelling. This latter group contains many valuable references to stories that are appropriate for various occasions.

COLLECTIONS OF STORIES

Abell, Elizabeth	First Book of Fairy Tales	Watt
Alexander, Beatrice	Famous Myths of the Golden Age	Random
Anderson, Hans Christian	Anderson's Fairy Tales	Grosset
A.C.E. International	Told Under the Green Umbrella	Macmillan
	Told Under the Blue Umbrella	"
	Told Under the Magic Umbrella	"
	Told Under Spacious Skies	"
Baker, Augusta	The Talking Tree and Other Stories	Lippincott
Baldwin, James	Favorite Tales of Long Ago	Dutton
Benson, Sally	Stories of the Gods and Heroes	Dial
Beston, Henry	Firelight Fairy Book	Little
Bowman, James C.	Pecos Bill	Whitman
Brock, Emma	Spooks and Spirits and Shadowy Shapes	Dutton
Bryant, Sara Cone	Stories to Tell to Children	Houghton

Bullfinch, Thomas	Mythology	Modern Library
Child Study Association	Holiday Story Book	Crowell
	Read-to-Me Story Book	"
	Read Me More Stories	"
	Read Me Another Story	"
Chase, Richard	Grandfather Tales	Houghton
	Jack Tales	"
	Jack and the Three Sillies	"
	Wicked John and the Devil	"
Dalgliesch, Alice	The Enchanted Book	Scribner
De La Mare, Walter	Told Again	Knopf
	Animal Stories	Scribner
Evans, Pauline	Family Treasury of Children's Stories (3 volumes)	Doubleday
Farjeon, Eleanor	The Little Book Room	Oxford
Felton, Harold	Legends of Paul Bunyan	Knopf
Fenner, Phyllis	Adventure Rage and Magical	Knopf
	Giants and Witches and a Dragon or Two	"
	Princesses and Peasant Boys	"
	Time to Laugh	Watts
	Yankee Doodle	"
Field, Rachel	American Folk and Fairy Tales	Scribner
Frost, Frances	Legends of the United States	Whittlesey
Fyleman, Rose	Tea Time Tales	Doubleday
Gaer, Joseph	Holidays Around the World	Little
Gale, Albert	Songs and Stories of the American Indians	Niel Kjos
Grimm, Brothers	Grimm's Fairy Tales	World
Jacobs, Joseph	The Fables of Aesop	Macmillan
Justus, May	Big Meeting and Other Festival Tales	Dutton
Kipling, Rudyard	Just So Stories	Doubleday
	Jungle Books, 1 and 2	"
Mabie, Hamilton	Folk Stories Every Child Should Know	Houghton
Mitchell, Lucy Sprague	Here and Now Story Book	Dutton
	Another Here and Now Story Book	"
	Believe and Make Believe	"

Pyle, Howard	The Wonder Clock	Harper
	Pepper and Salt	"
Sandburg, Carl	Rootabaga Stories	Harcourt
Scoggin, Margaret	Chucklebait	Knopf
	More Chucklebait	"
Sechrist,	Christmas Everywhere	Macrae
Elizabeth	Heigh-ho for Hallowe'en	Smith
	It's Time for Thanksgiving	"
Stockton, Frank	Ting-a-Ling Tales	Scribner
Wilde, Oscar	The Happy Prince and Other Fairy Tales	Putnam

STANDARD REFERENCES ABOUT STORYTELLING

Bryant, Sara Cone	How to Tell Stories to Children	Houghton
Jinnette, Isabella	Stories to Tell—A List of Stories with Annotations	Enoch Pratt Free Library
Royal, Claudia	Storytelling	Boardman Press
Sawyer, Ruth	The Way of the Storyteller	Viking
Shedlock, Marie	The Art of Story Telling	Appleton
Tooze, Ruth	Storytelling	Prentice-Hall
Wagner, J. A.	Children's Literature Through Storytelling	Wm. C. Brown

THE BLUE PITCHER

Henry A. Bamman

"It's a horrible, horrible day!" said Janie, and she thumped her heels on the floor. She was lying flat on her back, looking up at the ceiling of the living room, trying to count the tiny dots on the wall paper. "Oh, I wish I had something to do!"

Now, Janie wasn't very big, but then, she wasn't very small, either. She wasn't particularly tall, and she wasn't particularly short. In fact, she was just eight-big, and of course you know how big that is. All day long she had been wishing for something to do. Susan, her best friend next door, had the measles; Sally, who lived down the block, had gone to the zoo with her little brother. Just a few minutes ago, Mother had come in and said, as mothers often do, "Janie, I'm going to the store. Do you want to go with me?"

"No, thank you. I'd rather just stay here and do nothing," Janie had sighed.

So Mother had said, as mothers always do when they leave, "Now be a good girl while I'm gone, won't you?"

And Janie had replied, as anyone who is eight-big would reply, "Yes, Mother, I'll be good. There really isn't anything to do, anyway."

She had listened as Mother's footsteps went out the door and down the sidewalk to the front gate. She heard the gate squeak as it was opened, and then Mother's footsteps faded away until all Janie could hear was the tick-tick, tick-tick of the little clock on the mantle. Suddenly, the house seemed very quiet and very empty, and Janie rolled over on her side and looked up at the shelf high on the wall of the room. There, for the thousandth time, she saw it! Standing on the shelf, higher than anyone who is eight-big could reach, was the Blue Pitcher!

As long as Janie could remember, it had stood there, and as long as she could remember, she had wanted to touch it. But Mother had said, oh so many times, as mothers often do, "You may look at it, Janie, but you really must not touch it!"

The Blue Pitcher was an antique, and you know what that means, don't you? When something has belonged to great-grandmother and it is very, very old, it's an antique, of course. But the Blue Pitcher didn't look old. In fact, it was so shiny bright, with little white flowers marching all around it, and little white people dancing around its fat middle.

Now Janie sat up in the middle of the floor. She looked and looked at the Blue Pitcher, and then she had a wonderful thought! Not for a long time—at least not for two days or two weeks—had Mother said, "You mustn't touch it, Janie."

"I'm sure she wouldn't mind, now that I'm eight-big," said Janie. "After all, I can wash dishes without breaking them, and I do make my own bed now. I'm sure Mother wouldn't mind if I touched it just once," She jumped to her feet, pulled a chair over under the shelf, and quickly climbed up until her face was right next to the Blue Pitcher. "Oh!" she breathed, "It's more beautiful than I ever dreamed it would be!"

Slowly she put out her hand and touched it. It was so smooth and cool, and her fingers danced over the little white people and the smooth round flowers. "Oh, I want to hold it! I do! I do!" said Janie, and she put out both hands and clasped them around the Blue Pitcher. Lifting it gently, so very gently, she turned it around and around until she could see the little men and women and children as they danced all around the middle of the Blue Pitcher.

Just then, Janie did what anyone who is eight-big might do. She forgot that she was standing on the chair, took a big step, and CRASH! There was the Blue Pitcher, broken into one thousand and one pieces, lying on the floor.

Now what would you do if you were eight-big and all alone in the house and you had just broken your promise to your mother and broken the lovely Blue Pitcher that had belonged to great-grandmother? Why, you'd probably do just what Janie did. She sat down in the middle of the floor and cried! "What am I going to do? What am I going to do?" she cried.

"Janie!" It was a tiny voice, no bigger than the squeak of a mouse.

"Janie!" She lifted her head and looked all around the room. There it was again, "Janie!" She looked under the chair and up at the shelf; she peeked behind the door and under the cushions on the couch.

"Janie!" The voice was very near. Something moved on the table where Mother's sewing basket rested. The lip was pushed up, ever such a little bit, and peering out from under the lid were two of the blackest eyes you've ever seen!

Janie lifted the lid of the basket. You may not believe this, and I'm not sure that I do, either, but there was the tiniest Elf Man, sitting on a roll of yarn. He looked just as an Elf Man should, with a red coat and trousers, a tiny red cap, and red, red shoes! He looked at Janie, and he looked very stern!

"So, you've been a bad girl!" he said, nodding his head. "Now, stop that crying!" Oh, he was a stern Elf Man!

"Wh—Where did you come from?" asked Janie in her smallest voice.

"Never mind;" said the Elf Man. "Do you want me to help you, or don't you?"

Janie almost laughed, "But you're so little! How can you help me?"

The little Elf Man jumped out of the sewing basket and stood on top of the table. "Hurry up! Hurry up! There's no time to waste," he said. "Go to the kitchen and get a paper sack. Now!" Ah, he was a stern Elf Man!

Janie was back in a minute. The little Elf Man was sitting on the edge of the table. "Pick them up," he said. "Pick up all thousand and one pieces."

Quickly, Janie picked up the pieces of the Blue Pitcher and put them in the sack. Her fingers darted here and there. Oh, there were so many, many pieces to find, but finally she had all of them. Then she looked at the Elf Man.

"Well, help me down," he said, in his sternest voice. "I can't get down from here by myself!" Janie reached out her hand, and he hopped in. Gently, she put him down on the floor. He ran to the door, and turning around he said, "Well, come on! We have no time to waste!"

"But, where are we going?" asked Janie.

"Just don't ask too many questions!" said the Elf Man. "You come with me!"

Janie helped him down the steps, and he ran across the lawn to the corner of the garden. Suddenly he stood beside the high wall. He turned to Janie and shouted, "Hurry up! We're wasting time!"

"But, you can't go that way!" said Janie. "The gate is over there."

The Elf Man looked very, very stern. His black eyes looked through and through Janie. Then he turned to the wall. There, nodding in the breeze, was a big yellow tulip. The Elf Man looked up at the tulip, and very softly he said, "Quince! Quince! Quince!" Just like that! Janie gasped, because there beside the tulip, in the old garden wall, a tiny door opened, and the Elf Man stepped inside. "Come on, Janie, come on!"

Janie stepped up next to the wall. She looked down at the tiny door. "I can't! I'm too big!" she cried

"Oh my!" said the stern Elf Man. He stepped through the door, came very close to Janie, and putting out one tiny finger, he touched her. "Quince! Quince!" he said, so softly that only a whisper was heard.

Now, what do you suppose happened? Janie was getting smaller and smaller and smaller, until she was no taller than the Elf Man.

"Bring the sack!" said the Elf Man. Oh, he was stern!

"It's too big! I can't carry it!" cried Janie.

"Oh fiddles!" said the stern Elf Man. "Such a bother!" He stepped over to the sack, put out one tiny finger, and said, "Quince!" Just like that! And the sack was all at once so tiny that Janie could hardly see it. "Hurry, hurry!" said the Elf Man. "We have no time to waste!" He grabbed Janie's hand and pulled her through the little door.

It was very dark inside, and Janie could not see where they were going. The Elf Man held her hand, and all she could hear was the sound of their footsteps as they walked down a long, dark hallway. Then, far ahead, she saw a light. Within a minute, they were standing at a gate, and Janie couldn't believe what she saw!

Maybe you don't believe in fairies, and I'm not so sure that I do, either, but there, on the other side of the gate, were hundreds of fairies. There were blue fairies and pink fairies, yellow fairies and green fairies—all colors of fairies. They were dancing and singing under the nodding bluebells. The music from the bluebells, as they swayed in the breeze, was the most beautiful sound that Janie had ever heard.

The Elf Man pushed the gate open and stepped into the field where the fairies were dancing. He put his fingers in his mouth, and "Whee!" he whistled a shrill, shrill whistle. All of the fairies stopped dancing. They came running to where Janie and the Elf Man were standing. They looked at Janie in wonder. "What is it? What is it?" Janie heard them say.

The Elf Man smiled. "This is a little girl," he said, and he put his arm around Janie.

"Oh!" said the fairies. "A girl! A real little girl!" They came closer, and some of them put out their hands and touched Janie.

"She's a real little girl who is in real trouble," said the Elf Man sadly.

"Oh!" said the fairies. "In trouble. That's too bad, too bad." They shook their heads slowly.

"Do you think we can help her?" asked the Elf Man. "She's really a very good girl who forgot and made a mistake."

Now fairies are like boys and girls everywhere. They gathered in a group and Janie could hear them buzzing, buzzing, buzzing as they talked. Finally they came back to where the Elf Man was standing, and one of the fairies reached out her hand. "Let's see what we can do," she said, with a smile. "You sit down there, little girl." She pointed to a tiny hill, and Janie sat down under a nodding bluebell.

Fairies rushed everywhere. First there was clay to be pounded and sifted. There was water to be carried. "Splash! splash!" went the water as it was poured into the bowl of clay.

"Slurp! Slurp!" went the spoons as the fairies mixed something in the bowl.

There were so many fairies that Janie could not see what they were doing. A tiny fire was lighted in an oven. Someone called, "Bring the paint!" Something was lifted and Janie could see paint brushes moving quickly. Then the door of the little oven was opened and the fairies sat down to wait. Not a sound was heard except the tinkling of the bluebells. In a few minutes, the oven was opened again. "More paint!" someone called. Into the oven, out again; into the oven, out again.

All at once, the fairies were coming toward Janie, carrying something. The little Elf Man stepped forward and held out his hands. There, in his hands, was the tiniest blue pitcher that anyone has ever seen. Dancing all around its middle were little figures of men and women and children. Around the top and the bottom were smooth, white flowers.

"Put it in the sack!" said the Elf Man. He turned to Janie and his black eyes looked her through and through. "Hurry! We have no time to waste!" Oh, now he was stern again!

In the wink of an eye the pitcher was put in the sack, and the Elf Man handed it to Janie. He grabbed her hand and pulled her toward the tiny gate. "Come on!" he said. "Can't you hurry?"

Just as they reached the gate, Janie turned around. "Thank you, thank . . . . ." she started to say. But there were no fairies there. Only the bluebells were there, waving in the breeze. Janie listened carefully, but the bluebells weren't ringing. "Where did they go?" she cried.

The Elf Man pulled her through the gate, and they were walking down a long, dark hallway. Out of the door in the wall they stepped, and they were back in Janie's garden! They ran across the lawn, with the Elf Man pulling Janie so fast that she could hardly stay on her feet. They reached the steps at the front door of Janie's house.

"I can't get up!" cried Janie. "I'm too little."

"Such a bother!" said the Elf Man. But he reached out one tiny finger, touched Janie, and said, "Quince! Quince!" Just like that! And you know what happened, of course, before she could even breathe twice, there stood Janie, all of eight-big again!

"Well, help me up!" said the stern little Elf Man. Janie lifted him up the steps. They went through the door and into the living room. "Hurry!" said the Elf Man. "Put it on the shelf!" Oh, he was a stern Elf Man!

Janie gently lifted the tiny blue pitcher from the sack and climbed up on the chair. She placed the pitcher carefully, oh, so very carefully, on the shelf. "But it's too small!" she said, and she almost started to cry again.

"Oh, my!" said the Elf Man. "Such a bother! Pick me up!"

Janie picked him up in her hand and lifted him to the shelf. He reached out one tiny finger, touched the pitcher, and said, "Quince!" Just like that! Quickly, Janie stepped down from the chair and gently placed the Elf Man on the table beside the sewing basket. Then she looked at the shelf again.

"Oh, it's beautiful! It's wonderful! How did you ever do it?" she cried. There, just as it had been before, was the Blue Pitcher, looking so smooth and shiny with white flowers marching around it, and little white figures of men and women and

children dancing around its fat middle. "Oh, how can I ever
thank you? You've been so good to. . . ."

The little Elf Man was not on the table. Janie lifted the
lid of the sewing basket and looked under each ball of yarn,
but he wasn't there, either. She called and called to him, but
the only sound in the room was the tick-tick, tick-tick of the
little clock on the mantle. She ran out into the garden and
said, "Quince! Quince! Quince!" three times, to the big yellow
tulip beside the garden wall. But nothing happened. The yellow tulip just nodded its head in the breeze.

When mother came home from the store, she said, as
mothers usually do, "Well, Janie, did anything happen while
I was gone?"

"She'll never believe it if I tell her. Nobody would believe
it," thought Janie, so she sighed and said, "No, nothing much
happened. There just isn't anything to do today."

And to this day, Janie doesn't know whether to believe
this story or not. I'm not at all sure that I do. Do you?

Index